463

ping

pora-

THE
GOOD HOUSEKEEPING
COMPLETE
GUIDE TO
Traditional
American
Decorating

THE
GOOD HOUSEKEEPING
COMPLETE
GUIDE TO

Traditional American Decorating

KATHRYN KENT

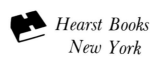
Hearst Books
New York

PRODUCED BY ROUNDTABLE PRESS, INC.
DESIGN: *Betty Binns Graphics/Madeleine Sanchez*
LINE ILLUSTRATIONS: *Ray Skibinski*

Library of Congress Cataloging in Publication Data
Kent, Kathryn.
 The Good housekeeping complete guide to traditional
American decorating.

 Includes index.
 1. Interior decoration—United States. I. Good
housekeeping (New York, N.Y.) II. Title.
NK2002.K46 1982   747.213   82-9280
ISBN 0-87851-212-8   AACR2

10 9 8 7 6 5 4 3 2 1

PRINTED IN THE UNITED STATES OF AMERICA

Contents

Introduction

Ever since the earliest colonists reached American shores, our country has been invaded by design ideas from every possible source. Jacobean furniture styles from England were brought by the first Pilgrims. Later waves of emigrants from England brought other English styles, and settlers from France, Holland, Scandinavia, Germany, Italy, and other countries also added to our rich and diverse design heritage.

Newcomers from every country recreated their native houses and furnishings as best they could, bringing as many household goods as possible, as well as seeds for their vegetable and flower gardens in the new land. And when pioneer men and women left the comparative safety of coastal settlements for the unknown wilderness, they, too, took along their familiar furnishings to maintain their own life-style insofar as they were able. As a result, we have inherited an enviable variety of choices in both architecture and decoration that enables us to live exactly as we want, in a degree of comfort unparalleled in history. And, like our ancestors, most of us tend to prefer the familiar traditional styles that have survived the test of time.

At present, a uniquely American style of living and dressing is emerging that is more relaxed with more attention to the way we *really* want to live and look rather than attempting to follow rigid decorating styles or trying to outdress our neighbors. Instead, we have a healthy new respect for basics and for simple, more functional designs that serve their purposes without frills or pretense. Today anything handmade is respected, whether you make it yourself or buy the work of a famous craftsman. And natural materials are admired for their intrinsic worth—the grain of wood; the weave of linen, cotton, wool, or silk; the gleam of silver; the form and glaze of clay.

There is also an overwhelming interest in folk art, both old and new—everything from quilts to whirling wind toys—all reflecting our back-to-basics approach to living and our enjoyment of simple pleasures.

This book is designed to help you create your own attractive and comfortable environment while basking in the safety of the familiar. The photographs are designed to give you hundreds of decorating ideas that you can adapt to your own home, and the text and line drawings explain, in simple terms, the basics of decorating.

Unlike Colonial times, gracious living is no longer a privilege of the wealthy. Today's technology makes possible, and affordable, the best in traditional design and styling. You can achieve any look you might want, and as you become your own decorator, you will be able to please your best client—yourself.

THE
GOOD HOUSEKEEPING
COMPLETE
GUIDE TO *Traditional*

American

Decorating

CHAPTER ONE

Traditional styles in America

What we call "traditional" derives, of course, from our heritage of American styles as they evolved through the years. In decorating, you may choose to recreate a specific historical style accurately or you may prefer to be eclectic in your selection of furnishings and accessories. Regardless of your preference, you will want to understand where traditional styles originated and how furniture—antique or reproduction—fits within the rich history of American styles in order to choose with intelligence based on sound knowledge. In this chapter the styles from early American to Victorian and mission are described and illustrated for easy reference; later styles, which are considered modern for the purposes of this book, are not included.

Period Styles

Furniture styles were traditionally named for the ruling monarch in seventeenth- and eighteenth-century Europe. But because of the decade or more it took for a new fashion to be transmitted from the old world to the new, stylistic nomenclature tends to be more complex in America. For example, American stylistic periods don't always coincide chronologically with the reigns of namesake European kings and queens, and styles may also be named for certain prominent furniture designers or corresponding periods of American history. Colonial styles were first imported by colonists from their mother

OPPOSITE PAGE:

Over backgrounds of soft yellow and white, authentically correct stencil designs add pattern to the floor and walls of this room. A simple leaf pattern wraps the tops of the walls, the window, and the chair rail, while weeping willow trees and pineapples (the symbol of hospitality) emphasize the fireplace wall.

Anatomy of a Chair

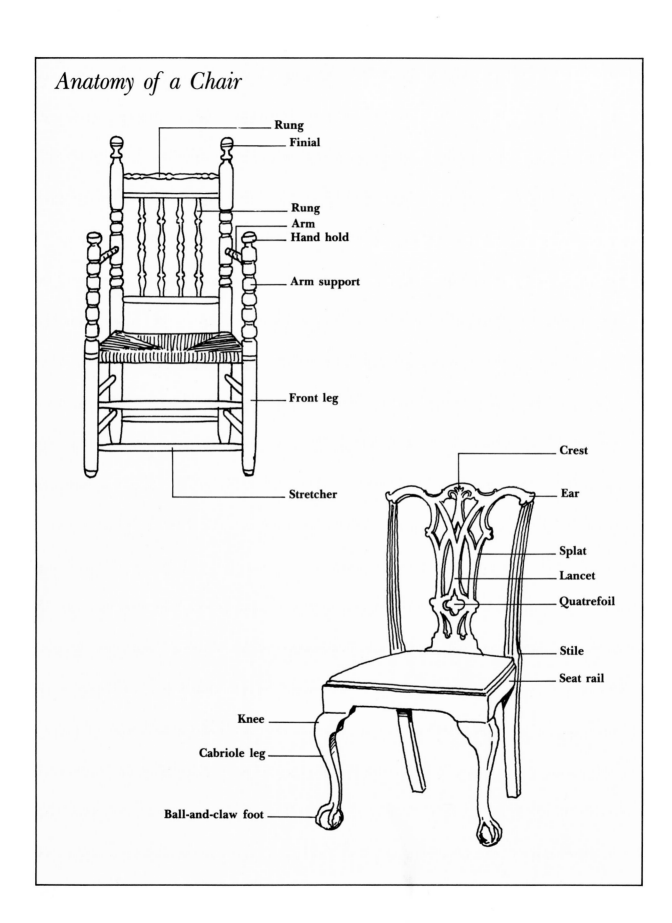

Rung
Finial
Rung
Arm
Hand hold
Arm support
Front leg
Stretcher
Crest
Ear
Splat
Lancet
Quatrefoil
Stile
Seat rail
Knee
Cabriole leg
Ball-and-claw foot

Back in 1942 Mrs. James Ward Thorne presented a unique collection of 37 "Rooms in Miniature" to the Art Institute of Chicago. Using a scale of one inch to a foot, it took more than ten years for skilled craftsmen, working under Mrs. Thorne's expert direction, to complete the monumental miniature project. The photographs shown throughout this chapter—taken from ten of the houses in the collection—display prime examples of their periods.

ABOVE:

This reconstruction of an early Colonial living room/kitchen is typical of Massachusetts architecture and furnishings from 1675 to 1700. The paneled walls, low-raftered ceiling, and leaded-glass casement windows are all reminiscent of homes left behind in England.

In simple early houses of this type the kitchen was also the living room, with every type of family activity gathered around the hearth—the only means of cooking and the only source of heat. High-backed settles near the fireplace were made in both adult and child sizes to help ward off drafts.

Stools and benches were more common than chairs, and armchairs were considered seats of honor. The multi-spindled armchair facing the trestle table is the type used by Elder Brewster, a leader of the Mayflower settlement; the other "Carver" armchair is named for a governor of the Plymouth Colony.

Braided floor mats are the earliest type recorded in this country; floors were most often covered with fine sand to absorb grease and tracked-in mud, all to be swept out and replaced with a fresh covering.

BELOW:

This miniature is an exact reproduction of a parlor in the Samuel Wentworth house built in Portsmouth, New Hampshire, in 1671; wall paneling and double-hung windows were added in 1710.

The early colonists brought memories of British styles in both architecture and furnishings to be translated by American craftsmen; the paneling and furniture are English in feeling but American in their actual execution.

country and later made by local craftsmen. Federal and empire styles followed our independence and the formation of our federal form of government.

Jacobean Furniture

The earliest American furniture has been termed Jacobean after James I, who ruled England from 1603 to 1625, when the first American colonies in Virginia and Massachusetts were founded. Pilgrim Century furniture is another term frequently used to describe these pieces, which were massive and sturdily constructed of oak, as were their European counterparts. (In fact, it is often difficult to distinguish between pieces made in Europe and America, although American carving was generally more primitive, and the furniture was frequently smaller to fit the limited dwelling spaces of early houses.)

Flat-carved strapwork, round-arched panels, turned legs, and bulbous feet characterize Jacobean furniture. Sometimes split spindles and applied, ebonized ornamental bits were used to decorate case pieces. Favored forms were court cupboards, press cupboards, and elaborately carved so-called Hadley and sunflower chests, all of which were essentially chests on feet.

Several types of chairs were in use during the seventeenth century: the Brewster chair, which had spindles in the back and below the arms; the Carver chair, with spindles only in the

In its early years Salem was a shipbuilding center, first sending out fleets of fishing vessels and, later, larger sailing ships that plied the East India trade. Early Salem houses were built by craftsmen trained to the demanding standards of shipwrights.

Paneling in this Salem dining room is of a type popular throughout the New England Colonies during the early part of the eighteenth century; decorative pilasters and arched cupboards of this type were often installed to "modernize" houses built in the previous century.

American-made furniture in the room closely follows the William and Mary style popular in England during the last quarter of the seventeenth century. The highboy evolved during this period of English design; the multi-legged lowboy and highboy are simplified versions of more ornate English models.

Chinese porcelain in the cupboard, a Chinese rug on the floor, and delft tiles surrounding the fireplace are typical of East India trade imports to the Colonies.

back; and the early wainscot chair, with a solid flat-carved back and a plank seat. Gateleg and trestle tables were also popular at the time. The most common seat was the joined or "joint" stool, which resembles a miniature trestle table.

William and Mary

Between 1690 and 1725 the dominant style in America was called William and Mary after the Dutch monarch William of Orange, who acceded to the throne of England in 1689 with his wife, Mary. Elaborate turnings, carvings in high relief, baroque scrolled crests on chairs, tapered scroll feet (called Spanish feet) on chairs, and bulbous bun feet on chests were all typical of the period.

On formal pieces, caning and japanning—a polychrome lacquer finish—gave evidence to the new influence of Oriental design, introduced through the China trade. Trumpet-turned legs on tables and chests were joined by x-shaped, flat-carved stretchers. Lowboys, highboys, drop-front desks, and wing chairs first came into fashion in this period. Pendant teardrop pulls were favored for drawer hardware. Daybeds were a common form, often having six or eight legs joined by flat, curved stretchers. The Kas, a massive painted chest or wardrobe, was a popular regional form in New York and Pennsylvania; it continued to be made through much of the eighteenth century. During the William and Mary period, walnut or other hardwoods veneered with walnut burl or maple were the favored woods.

Queen Anne Style

By 1720 a major stylistic change was underway. Named for the British monarch who reigned from 1702 to 1714, the Queen Anne style was distinguished by fluid, simple curving shapes exemplified best by the cabriole leg, which was first seen in

Long before the revolution, prosperous plantation owners in the South lived a luxurious life that equaled, or even surpassed, their wealthy British counterparts. The elegantly paneled drawing room pictured here is based on a room in Wilton, a 1754 mansion built in Virginia for William Randolph III. In 1935 Wilton was moved to West Hampton near Richmond and is now the property of the Society of Colonial Dames of America.

Furniture in the room is mostly Queen Anne, a graceful early-eighteenth-century style that remained popular in the Colonies until well beyond the midcentury. The small table holding the bird cage is an excellent example of Queen Anne hallmarks—cabriole legs ending in pad feet and a carved apron. The japanned highboy with chinoiserie decoration reflects the spread of popular "Chinese taste" from Europe to America.

Fluted pilasters and arches flanking the marble mantelpiece are true to the original construction; the elaborate ceiling plaster work was probably added at a later date.

France around 1700. Pieces termed Queen Anne in America were known as George I and George II furniture in England. The style remained popular here through the first half of the century.

Queen Anne chairs generally had cabriole legs, pad feet, fiddle- or vase-shaped back splats, and hoop-shaped or gently rounded crests. Many seating pieces were upholstered, including the wing chair, which became very popular at this time. Tea tables—reflecting the vogue for tea drinking that began in the 1730s—and card tables were other new forms of the period. The high chest, or highboy, also came into its own during this time, particularly in America where it was often decorated with a broken-arch pediment and shell carving, the favored motif of the period.

Regional characteristics in American furniture, particularly in the form and the type of wood preferred, were quite pronounced during the Queen Anne period. Boston-made furniture, often of cherry or maple, is simple and usually has elongated cabriole legs that are sometimes joined by stretchers. New York furniture is sturdy, squat, and squarish with deeply etched carving. Philadelphia chairs of the period are beautifully carved, often having trifid (or triangle-shaped pad) feet in front. Walnut was the predominate wood used in New York, Pennsylvania, and the South.

Chippendale

By the late 1750s, an anglo-French style named for British furniture designer Thomas Chippendale, whose *Gentlemen and Cabinet-Maker's Director* of 1754 codified and popularized the fashion, was dominant in the American colonies. So-called Chippendale furniture had three distinctly different sources of design inspiration: the French rococo, with its curvilinear form, carved S and C scrolls, asymmetrical vegetal carving, and shell patterns; the Chinese, who inspired fretwork detailing and pagoda motifs; and neogothic, seen in chairs with pierced backs

Distinctive styles in both architecture and furniture design were developed in Rhode Island during the early part of the nineteenth century. This room reproduces a parlor in the Waterman House, built about 1820 in Warren, Rhode Island.

Architectural details—the mantel, door heads, molding, and dado—combine an earlier broken-reverse-curve pediment with designs influenced by the English architect Robert Adam, who was partial to floral swags, garlands, and bowknots. All are distinctly American interpretations of European design.

The impressive secretary, made in two pieces with brass carrying handles on both, is a fine example of John Goddard's unique Rhode Island style, with block front drawers and finely carved shells and finials. The chairs and card table are outstanding examples of American rendering of Chippendale designs. An Oriental-design needlepoint rug covers the floor, and a pair of porcelain urns and a portrait decorate the mantel.

and case furniture with pointed arches and mullions. Earlier pieces have Queen Anne-type cabriole legs; older Chippendale styles have straight front legs.

American Chippendale furniture may be classic in its simplicity, with restrained ornament and graceful lines, or it may be quite rococo, with naturalistic carving, pierced splats, and ball-and-claw feet. The latter were often added to Thomas Chippendale designs by Philadelphia cabinetmakers.

Evolving from the early settle, the sofa was introduced in this period. Usually it had a serpentine-curved or "camel" back and either ball-and-claw feet or straight "Marlborough" legs. Pembroke tables (with small drop leaves), tea tables, kettle stands, knee-hole desks or dressing tables, and block-front chests of drawers were popular forms of the Chippendale period. The massive breakfront was found most often in the South. City cabinetmakers like the Townsend-Goddard family of Newport—famed for their block-front shell-carved case furniture—were imitated by their rural counterparts, and a lively and simplified style called Country Chippendale was the result. Mahogany was the favored wood of the high-style cabinetmakers during this period, although regional artisans in the north relied on local woods such as cherry, maple, and pine and those in the South, on walnut, cedar, and cypress.

Windsor Furniture

During the second half of the eighteenth century and well into the nineteenth, Windsor chairs and benches—made from spindles joined to a plank seat with turned hardwood legs—were widely popular in America. The name derived from the English town of Windsor, where the furniture was originally made and sold during the seventeenth century. Resilient hickory or ash wood was used to make spindles for American Windsor chairs and settees, which were often painted to achieve a practical and

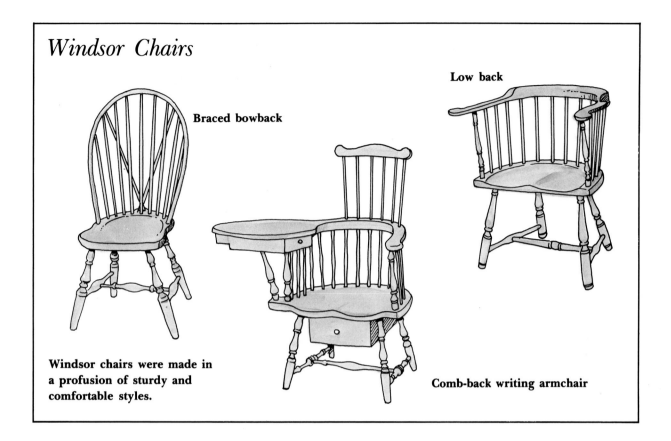

Windsor Chairs

Braced bowback

Low back

Windsor chairs were made in a profusion of sturdy and comfortable styles.

Comb-back writing armchair

durable finish. Windsor seating pieces complemented simple country Chippendale furniture in many village and rural homes of the late eighteenth century.

The Federal Period

By the 1770s a revolution in furniture design was under way, led by English architect Robert Adam, who, like others of his generation, was influenced by the recent archeological discoveries at Herculaneum and Pompeii. The curving forms and elaborate rococo ornamentation of earlier times were abandoned in favor of the simpler, more delicate, and more formal straight lines of neoclassic design. Tapered round or square legs, delicate flutings and moldings, inlay and light carving in various classical motifs, such as the Greek key or bellflower, were hallmarks of the style.

George Hepplewhite, who wrote *The Cabinet-Maker and Upholsterer's Guide* in 1788, and Thomas Sheraton, whose *Cabinetmaker and Upholsterer's Drawing Book* appeared between 1791 and 1794, helped to popularize neoclassic furniture. Hepplewhite design favored slender, tapering square legs, ending in a spade foot, and the decorative inlay of classic motifs in light wood. Chair backs are often shield-shaped or, less frequently, heart or balloon-shaped. Sheraton style pieces,

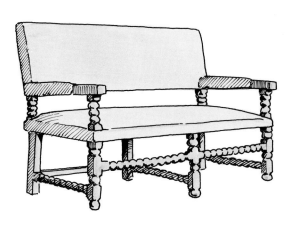
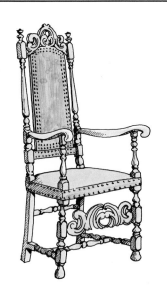

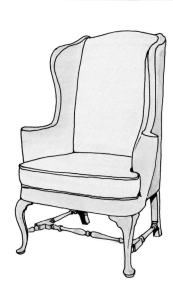

Jacobean
1650–1690

Jacobean, also known as Pilgrim Century, was the first style to reach our shores. It is distinguished by tables and seating pieces with turned legs and stretchers, chests that are decorated with applied split spindles and ebonized ornamental bits and sit on bulbous feet. The turned Carver chair pictured here is the type brought from England by John Carver, the first governor of the pilgrims' newly-formed Plymouth Colony in Massachusetts.

William and Mary
1690–1720

William and Mary chairs display elaborate turning and deep carving with ornately scrolled crests. Wing chairs became fashionable during this period; the example pictured shows tapered Spanish feet typical of the style. The highboy is distinguished by such William and Mary features as trumpet-turned legs with bun feet, flat-carved curvaceous stretchers (often X-shaped with a finial in the center), and pendant tear-drop drawer pulls.

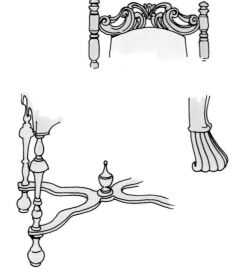

Queen Anne
1720–1750

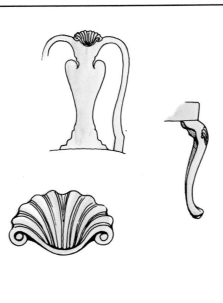

Queen Anne furniture has gracefully curving cabriole legs, usually with pronounced knees and pad feet. The chairs have vase- or fiddle-shaped splat backs with rounded crests and turned stretchers. During this period, a more graceful version of the William and Mary upholstered armchair became very popular. American-made Queen Anne highboys often featured a broken pediment embellished by three flame-carved finials. Shell carving was a favorite motif.

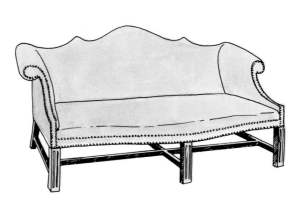

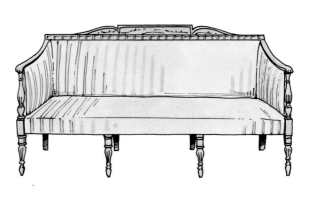

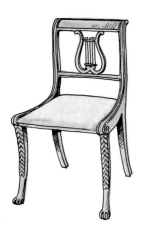
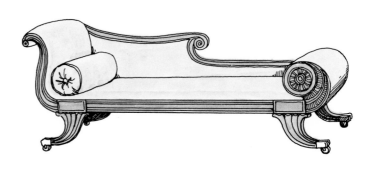

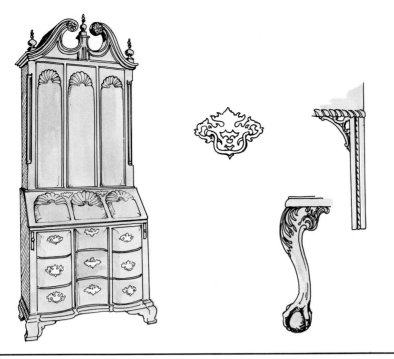

Chippendale
1750–1775

Chippendale's inspiration came from three major sources: French rococo, Chinese, and previous English styles. Philadelphia cabinetmakers are credited with adding a ball-and-claw foot to the ornately carved pieces they adapted from Thomas Chippendale's design book. During this period the settee evolved into a sofa; shown here is an American version of Chippendale's classic "camel" back sofa as well as a side chair and block-front secretary with typical bracket feet.

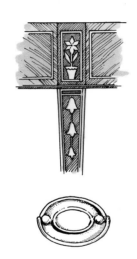

Federal
1785–1820

Federal styles in America were greatly influenced by design books published by Hepplewhite and Sheraton during the late eighteenth century. The delicately carved shield-back chair with slender legs and spade feet, and the sideboard with tapered legs and curving corners are signatures of Hepplewhite's designs. The typical Sheraton sofa pictured has an ornamental crest over a rectangular back and columns, projecting beyond curving arms, ending in carved legs.

Empire
1820–1840

American Empire furniture reflected the popularity of Napoleon's French Empire styles inspired by classical Greek, Roman, and Egyptian designs. Named for the French Mme. Recamier, the chaise longue pictured is based on the design of an early Roman couch. The lyre-back chair is typical of Duncan Phyfe's adaptations of classical motifs so popular during this period. Architectural pillars often adorn chests and sideboards, and animalistic motifs, such as the hairy paw feet, were common.

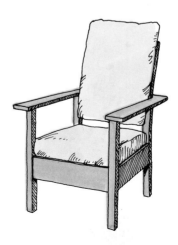

Victorian
1840–1870s

Victorian furniture styles encompass three major types. The first was a revival of Gothic forms based on medieval architectural ornamentation, such as the side chair with a round back simulating a cathedral's rose window. The next, a curving rococo style with naturalistic carving of grapes and roses that is best exemplified by the John Belter tête-à-tête sofa. The third, Renaissance Revival, adopted a more solid, symmetrical look, as the cabinet.

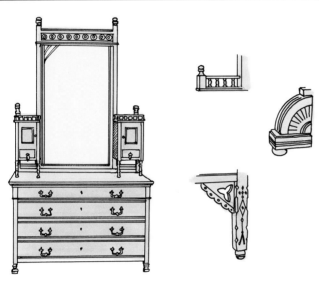

Reform (Eastlake)
1868–1880s

Reform furniture styles were instigated by the English architect Charles Locke Eastlake who objected to the structural weakness of Victorian rococo pieces. Instead, he advocated a return to sturdy rectangular Gothic shapes with incised geometric designs and other simple ornaments. In America, spindled elements augmented Eastlake's incised decoration on Renaissance Revival forms. The pieces pictured here are prime examples of American Eastlake.

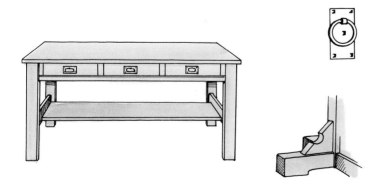

Reform (Mission)
1890–1915

Mission styles began in protest to shoddy machine-made goods—a revolt led by William Morris in mid-nineteenth-century England and continued by the Arts and Crafts Movement in America before and after the turn of the twentieth century. In this country, Gustav Stickley, a leader of the revolt, used fumed oak to create straight-lined furniture with honestly obvious joints and simple hardware, expressive of Stickley's mission to improve design and craftsmanship.

Fancy Chairs

Stencil-decorated Hitchcock chairs are still being made in their original and charming styles.

in a similar neoclassic tradition, were tempered by the influences of the Louis XVI and French Directoire period and have tapering round legs that are sometimes reeded. The chairs have rectangular backs enclosing a lyre-shaped splat, interlaced arches, or other open decorative devices. Another Sheraton signature is the use of columns that project at the corners of a piece of furniture. Formal dining, which assumed new importance during this period, lead to the introduction of the sideboard and sectional dining table. Another fashionable item was the tambour desk.

In America variations on Hepplewhite and Sheraton designs were produced by many fine cabinetmakers including Samuel McIntire of Salem, Massachusetts, and Duncan Phyfe of New York City. Such pieces are generally categorized as Federal and were made until about 1815. The favored woods were mahogany, satinwood, and other native or imported light woods, often inlaid with wood of a contrasting color or grain.

Fancy Furniture

Gilded and painted variations of Sheraton seating pieces were widely produced in the United States in the first half of the nineteenth century. Sometimes elements of Windsor furniture—back splints split and carved to resemble arrows—were incorporated into this type of design. Such "fancy chairs" could be quite formal in appearance, like the fine painted examples from Baltimore, or they could be "countrified," like the

unpretentious mass-manufactured fancy chairs and settees turned out by Lambert Hitchcock at his factory in Connecticut from the 1820s to the early 1840s.

American Empire: 1815–1840

By 1820 the interpretation of classicism in furniture design had become much more literal. In part, this vogue derived from Napoleon's Egyptian campaigns and the subsequent rage for Greco-Roman Egyptianate furniture that spread throughout the fashionable salons of his empire.

In America chairs, tables, and cabinets grew more massive. Wide expanses of flame-grained mahogany veneer were embellished with ornamentation and carvings such as hairy paw feet, dolphins, sphinxes, and griffins. Cabinetmakers of French descent in Philadelphia and New York, like Anthony Quervelle and Charles-Honoré Lannuier, took the style to its extreme. The later work of Duncan Phyfe—with its broader curves and more substantial lines—also represented empire furniture at its best. But improvements in furniture-making technology—veneer cutters and new saws—enabled simpler versions of the

The parlor in Eagle House, built in Haverhill, Massachusetts, in 1818, is a prime example of the luxurious and gracious decorating that prevailed during the Federal period—a time when many New England merchants became prosperous as a result of their shipping interests.

In this, the most formal room in the house, scenic wallpaper from France is a suitable background for American adaptations of Hepplewhite shield-back chairs plus a Sheraton-style sofa and high-back armchair. Delicate candlestands holding elegant silver candlesticks flank the tambour desk; beside the bookcase, a gilded candle sconce on the wall incorporates a convex mirror to add further reflected candlelight.

The delicately detailed mantelpiece and hearth accessories, including the fire screen on a stand, are typical of the period. Fringe-trimmed rich damask is used for the simple yet formal window treatment of tied-back draperies and a swag.

This period representation is based on a drawing room in Andalusia, a historic house in Bensalem Township, Pennsylvania, which was remodeled in 1834. At the height of the Greek revival movement, many older houses were "updated" to add the popular classic columns and temple facades—even including versions of caryatids, the female figures supporting the marble mantel.

It was during this late Sheraton-Empire period that Duncan Phyfe evolved his own graceful version of the prevailing style. In this drawing room, two chairs and a pair of tables show his refinement of the lyre motif; the backs of two other chairs are a delicate repeat of their x-shaped legs. The settee is Samuel McIntire's American version of a Sheraton design.

The crystal chandelier, "bulls-eye" mirrored wall sconces, and finely wrought candleholders on the mantel are typical of the elegance of the period.

style to be economically produced for a wide range of consumers. This so-called pillar and scroll furniture—named for the scroll-shaped supports beneath tables and cabinets and the pillars that framed the sides of chests and sideboards—was made well into the 1840s. Variations of the Greek Klismos chair and the Roman curule chair were also popular throughout the period.

Victorian: Revival and Reform Styles

During Queen Victoria's long reign, from 1837 to 1901, a succession of popular furniture styles graced America's homes. Several of these styles derived elements of form and decoration from earlier periods. The first of the Victorian revival styles was the Gothic Revival (1835–1845), which took its inspiration from medieval architecture: arches, crockets, finials, tracery, and pierced work were translated into rosewood, walnut, and mahogany. Elements of the Gothic Revival were sometimes combined with the corkscrew-turned posts and stretchers that characterized the so-called Elizabethan Revival, a style that enjoyed a brief vogue during the 1840s. By the early 1850s, Rococo Revival, with its many curves and naturalistic carved grapes and roses, had come into fashion. John Henry Belter's name has become synonymous with Rococo Revival, although many other cabinetmakers worked in the style. Belter learned how to glue together many thin layers of wood (a process called lamination) and how to shape them into curving forms in a steam-heated mold or "caul." He then carved this rosewood laminate into intricate forms, creating the style that most Americans envision when they think of Victorian furniture.

The nation's mood changed during the dark days of Civil War, and by 1865, the heavy forms of the Renaissance Revival

This fashionable Victorian parlor reproduces a room in the New York City brownstone home where Theodore Roosevelt spent his childhood. Ornate molding, fussy window treatments, heavy gilt-framed mirrors, "busy" patterned wallpaper, and carpet are all typical of furnishings in the Victorian revival styles.

This set of delicately carved rosewood furniture is in the style of New York's John Henry Belter, who created his own version of Rococo English designs—a version that surpassed the best British efforts and is now considered classic.

In the homes of the wealthy, Victorian niceties also included an ornate gaslight ceiling fixture, glass Wardian cases protecting lasting arrangements of wax flowers, at least one marble bust, and a rubber plant at the window.

seemed more appropriate for American parlors than the ornate, curving excesses of the light-hearted prewar Rococo. Renaissance Revival furniture was made primarily of walnut. It tended to be symmetrical with a raised central pediment or crest flanked by lower side elements. Applied ornamentation and gilding appeared frequently. Chairs had turned legs and ornate back crests, and sofas were often tripartite, or designed in a three-part configuration. Renaissance Revival remained fashionable through the 1870s.

Reform Furniture

By the middle of the nineteenth century, a reform movement arose in reaction to these excesses of historic revival design. The curving, "constructively weak" forms of the Rococo Revival were particularly distasteful to English architect Charles Locke Eastlake, whose *Hints on Household Taste,* published in many editions on both sides of the Atlantic beginning in 1868, became the bible of design reform. Eastlake favored simple, functional rectilinear furniture of "obvious construction," simple orna- ment, functional strap hinges, and incised geometric decoration. The illustrations in his book tended toward the Gothic, but in America, much of the factory-made "Eastlake" furniture of the late 1870s and 1880s consisted of Eastlake-type geometric- incised decoration and turned spindled elements superimposed on basically Renaissance Revival forms.

In the same reformist vein, another mid-nineteenth-century Englishman, William Morris, spearheaded a revolt against shoddy machine-made goods and advocated a return to the craft principles of the Middle Ages. His philosophy became the backbone of the Arts and Crafts Movement that flourished in America during the decades just before and after the turn of the

In 1540, Coronado left Mexico to lead an expedition into what is now Santa Fe. Although no visual trace remains of this early attempt to expand the Spanish Empire, old missions established around San Antonio are evidence of the Spanish padres who were pioneers in our western civilization and left their mark on our culture.

This model of a New Mexican dining room is based on a hallway in the ancient palace of Spanish governors in San An- tonio. Architecturally the room is essentially Spanish in feeling but built with native Pueblo Indian methods and materials. The corner fireplace, three-foot thick walls made of sun-dried adobe brick, and ceiling of undressed logs interlaced with smaller saplings are characteristic of adobe houses throughout the Southwest.

The spindled cupboard, straight-lined chest, trestle table, and leather-seated chairs are Spanish in character; the three rush-seated and paint-decorated chairs are typically Mexican.

American Furniture Variations

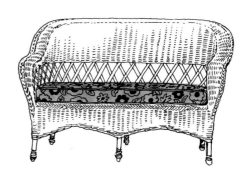

WICKER

Immensely popular during the Victorian era, wicker furniture is now returning to favor.

BENTWOOD

Brought to America by the Austrian Thonet brothers in 1873, bentwood furniture is still popular.

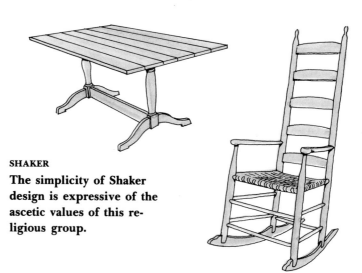

SHAKER

The simplicity of Shaker design is expressive of the ascetic values of this religious group.

twentieth century. In furniture making, perhaps its best exponent was Gustav Stickley, whose shop turned out sturdy, straight-lined pieces of fumed oak with straight-forward mortis-and-tenon joints, known as mission furniture in recognition of Stickley's mission to improve standards of design and craftsmanship. Stickley had many imitators, and mission furniture was manufactured widely in the period before World War I.

American Furniture Variations

During the nineteenth century, technology had a great impact on furniture design, as craftsmen learned new, economical ways to cut, join, and shape wood. Michael Thonet, an Austrian, discovered a revolutionary means of bending wood in the 1830s, and by the 1850s his sons were turning out hundreds of mass-produced bentwood chairs in their Vienna factory. After the Thonet brothers opened a shop in New York in 1873, their furniture became widely popular in the United States and remained so for several decades.

Wicker furniture, a mainstay of the Victorian household, could be found in every room from the nursery to the porch. Wicker lent itself to mass production: By century's end a number of factories were specializing in wicker tables, chairs, settees, baby carriages, dressing tables, and other forms. These pieces were often painted and bedecked with ribbon bows, lending a light touch to the eclectic room arrangements of late Victorian homes.

In marked contrast to the highly ornamental quality of much nineteenth-century furniture is the sheer simplicity of Shaker design. The Shakers were an ascetic communal sect who settled in various parts of the United States early in the nineteenth century. They believed all ornament to be superfluous and sinful; fine craftsmanship and practical design were, for them, evidences of piety. The tables, chairs, rockers, hanging pegs, and built-in cabinets they made for their own community use are therefore masterpieces of simplicity and functionalism.

In 1774 Ann Lee established the first American branch of the Shaker religious sect in New Lebanon, New York. By the early nineteenth century, community houses had been created in Pennsylvania, Ohio, Kentucky, and Indiana. This model represents a common room in a Shaker community house of about 1800.

An offshoot of the Quaker religion, Shaker "believers" were devoted to their motivating principle: "Hands to work and hearts to God." Adherence to this belief created hardworking and devoted craftsmen who emphasized economy of design and fitness of purpose without ornamental addition of any kind.

Often considered the forerunner of modern design, Shaker furniture is a distinct American style without a trace of European influence. The room pictured here demonstrates the spare, clean lines of Shaker furniture, the functional and economical design of their wood stove, and their ingenious invention of wall-hung pegged boards used to hold anything from hats to chairs.

Some Common Furniture Terms

SPLAT BACK
A central support, connecting the top rail to the seat of a chair. The splat can be solid or pierced.

BANISTER OR BALUSTER BACK
A chair back constructed with split balusters set vertically, round side facing to the back, between the top rail and seat.

PAD FOOT
An oval shaped foot set on a disc, generally used on a Queen Anne cabriole leg.

FIDDLE SPLAT
A solid splat for a chair back whose profile and concave curved shape resembles the contours of a violin.

LADDER BACK
A chair back with horizontal slats or rails.

BALL-AND-CLAW FOOT
A bird's claw holding a ball flattened on the bottom, commonly used on a Chippendale cabriole leg.

VASE SPLAT
A flat splat shaped in the form of an urn.

PLANK SEAT
A chair seat formed by a flat, single board.

BUN FOOT
A large ball-shaped foot, flattened on top and bottom, used to support tables, chairs, and chests.

During the late nineteenth century, the Shakers also made chairs and some other objects for sale to the general public; these are simply turned and usually have tape-woven seats.

Primitive Country

So much American furniture that is popular in today's decorating derives from what was made by or for country folk for their own use at work, rest, or play. Within this category you will find a charmingly naive approach to useful design. Because frontier

SPADE FOOT
A square spade-shaped foot, used on a straight, tapered leg.

TURNING
A length of wood that has been shaped into curves on a lathe.

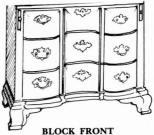

BLOCK FRONT
A bowed front with concave sides and a convex center.

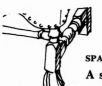

SPANISH FOOT
A scroll foot with curving vertical ribs, generally used on a turned leg.

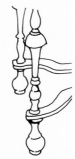

TRUMPET TURNING
A turned form whose profile resembles the shape of a trumpet turned upside down.

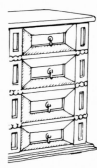

PANEL
A board fitting into grooves and enclosed with molding to create a recessed or raised surface.

CROCKETS
A projecting carved decoration.

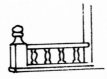

SPINDLES
Slender, turned rods.

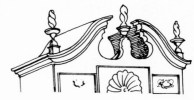

PEDIMENT
In furniture, the triangular decoration above a tall chest, bookcase, or mirror. A broken pediment is one lacking the apex of the triangle.

homes were usually small, often a one-room log cabin with a sleeping loft for children, dual-purpose furniture was highly desirable: hutch tables that converted to chairs, beds that folded into cupboards or trundle beneath higher beds when not in use during the day. Basically, early American pioneer furniture is a simplified version of styles used by wealthy landowners and the urban middle class. In this naively charming category you will find pieces that are usually of solid pine or maple, such as sturdy six-board chests, settees, cupboards, trestle tables, dry sinks, all-wood chairs, or chairs with seats woven of rush or rope rather than upholstery.

CHAPTER TWO

Discovering your own style

Decorating your home is a little like falling in love: It fills you with excitement, anticipation, and delight. And while it sets you to daydreaming, it also makes you more aware of everything around you—of colors and textures and shapes and of how these can be combined to produce exactly the effect you want, whether you're slipcovering a chair or decorating a whole house.

Still, these pleasurable feelings are sometimes tinged with doubt. How do you make a choice among the many possibilities open to you? How do you even know what all the possibilities are? It's true that a wrong choice here is one of life's lesser disasters. But it is a disaster nonetheless, and it's more deplorable because it is so easily prevented.

For decorating is not the mystery it is sometimes made out to be. If you can put together an attractive costume—a dress, a scarf, a pair of shoes—you'll have no trouble making your home a pleasant and comfortable place to live in, one that will please your family and impress your friends. The tools you need are simply a few general principles and a lot of specific facts. This book is designed to give you both, plus a look at the many resources available to you whatever project you decide to undertake. But that's not all.

The best of all possible ways of decorating, for you and your family, is a way that is entirely and individually yours. Consequently, this book's main purpose is to help you develop confidence in your own taste and judgment. It is here that the

OPPOSITE PAGE:

Friendly informality and easy hospitality are evident throughout this open-plan house. Blue predominates, cheered by pink and warmed by the natural tones of knotty-pine paneling. Furnishings are an eclectic mix of contemporary upholstered pieces combined with antiques and reproductions.

illustrations can be especially helpful. First of all, they cover a great variety of traditional styles. Among them you are sure to find several that more or less reflect the way you like to live and your budget.

But more than that, these pictures are planned to teach you a new way of looking, to train your eye to see the rules behind all good decorating. *Those* rules are not cut-and-dried dos and don'ts that may or may not apply to your particular situation. They result from a natural feeling for the relationships among the many elements—color, pattern, texture, and so forth—that combine to produce a handsome room, apartment, or house. Once you learn to spot these relationships and apply them to your own problems, decorating your home will become the exhilarating and successful experience it's supposed to be.

Begin at the Beginning

Begin by thinking about the way you live and how you like to entertain. Would you classify your life-style as casual or formal, or somewhere in between? Are you completely family oriented or do you often entertain friends and business associates? Do you enjoy collecting and its inevitable accumulation of treasures, or do you prefer the easy maintenance of a spare, down-to-basics environment? Is your home one where there is a place for everything and everything is (or should be) in its place? Or does your family live all over the house, with toys, books, and magazines everywhere contributing to a look of cheerful clutter? When the weather permits, do you do a good deal of living outdoors? Is your way of life child oriented or directed toward adult interests? Or is it a happy combination of both? How much entertaining do you do, and what kind? Does your family do things together, or is each one of you a rugged individualist? What are the main traffic patterns in your home? Is it a reasonably permanent abode, or do you expect to move to a new home in a few years?

This is just a sampling of the kinds of questions you should know the answers to before you even begin collecting swatches. A decorating scheme is a good one only if it works. And to work it must add to the pleasure and comfort of every member of the household. Discuss your plans with those who share this space with you. You may find that they can contribute ideas and insights you have overlooked. Once you have analyzed your basic needs you will have a much better idea of which style is best for you.

Temperament Makes the Difference

At the opposite extreme from the homey feeling of a New England kitchen or a New Mexican adobe house are styles modeled after those favored by the aristocracy in periods when

If quilts are your passion—especially if you make them—they add an exciting profusion of pattern and color to your house. Special handiwork is evident in this quilt-filled bedroom with new work in progress on the quilt rack at right.

In this comfortable old farmhouse living room, an antique grocery store bin, with its original display shelves filled with jars of dried food of various types, creates a fascinating focal point. An old pine chest serves as a coffee table for a pair of tuxedo loveseats.

Tidiness and a strong contemporary feeling are evident in this lofty apartment with separate areas defined for living, cooking, and eating. Kitchen activity is hidden behind free-standing shelves filled with collectibles. The checkerboard motif is repeated by pillows on the upholstered pieces. In the dining area, an antique hutch table and four early thumb-back chairs have been placed under a many-armed antique chandelier.

life was more leisurely and more ordered, at least for the upper classes. These periods and styles vary widely in origin and flavor, from the formal styles of the Colonial period to the simple, classic lines of mission furniture that originated in the mid-nineteenth century. The family that likes to entertain formally, that makes a habit of traditions like afternoon tea, that enjoys the pleasures of conversation and other quiet pursuits often finds itself happiest in a more formal setting. It can be recreated authentically with fine antiques or, at a more moderate cost, by using the excellent reproductions of earlier styles that are now available.

Because of the overwhelming interest in nostalgia, manufacturers are now offering excellent reproductions of almost everything from our American past—furniture, fabrics, floor and wall coverings, lamps, and accessories of all types—so once you have decided on your particular style you need not be limited to more costly antiques.

You can be as grand or as simple as you like: For example, American colonial styling ranges from the elegance of the restored Governor's palace in Colonial Williamsburg to the far less opulent homes of the Pilgrims and other settlers in each of the original colonies.

Perhaps you would feel more at home with early American—a style that encompasses simpler versions of more elegant colonial pieces. Our own Federal period is one that also allows for any degree of formality you might want to achieve. But if completely casual is your way of life, country primitive will appeal to you, as will its easy maintenance in these days of few if any servants.

Between the most formal and the most informal ways of decorating there is an almost infinite series of gradations and variations. Just as modern styling isn't confined to casual settings, so a fondness for the traditional look doesn't mean you must force your family's behavior into an unnaturally rigid mold.

Some period styles vary in degree of formality according to the patterns and textures used with them. Brocades, velvets, silks, and satins, in classic patterns and traditional motifs, give a room a grander air than one in which fabrics equally appropriate but sturdier—printed cottons and linens, or wools, perhaps—are used.

Nor is there any law of decorating that says you must furnish a traditional room in a completely traditional way. Some of the most interesting decorating schemes, as well as the most comfortable, are achieved by mixing periods or combining the old and the new.

If, like most of us, you find the familiarity of traditional styles comforting—zero in on whatever pleases you the most. Perhaps you have inherited a few family pieces and would like to plan your decorating around them. Consider your cherished possessions as a beginning but not necessarily the end. You can be as eclectic as you like; mix or match as you choose, but

unless your rooms are very large always keep scale in mind—the size of your rooms will more or less dictate the size of your furniture. An enormous highboy touching the ceiling in a small room will dominate and dwarf everything else, including you.

Your Budget

Whether your decorating project is one room or an entire house, decide on your budget and establish priorities. Don't be stampeded into costly mistakes by trying to do everything at once; the longer you take, the more money you will be able to add to your budget. Instead, begin with an overall plan and purchase according to priority. Perhaps your living-room sofa is beyond repair or your worn bedroom rug should be replaced. Decide which need is the most immediate, and shop with your ultimate decorating scheme in mind.

While shopping for any major furniture purchase, the rule of thumb is to buy the style that appeals the most in the best quality you can afford; it will serve you best and please you for many years to come.

If uncomplicated country living is your dream, a primitive kitchen might be for you. Authentic color on this cabinetry approximates early buttermilk paint; base cabinets and the free-standing cupboard are Shaker in their simplicity; Shaker-style pegs near the ceiling hold a variety of kitchen items.

If country is your preferred style, you can have it wherever you live. In this big city apartment, a pencil-post bed, an antique corncrib holding books beside the wing chair, rag rugs on the floor, a scattering of weathervanes and early toys all add up to a sophisticated country look.

Consider Color, Pattern, and Texture

Think about color and what it can do for you. The color chapter in this book will explain the so-called mysteries of color, but your ultimate choices should be geared to your own preferences. Color speaks its own language and creates its own mood. It can warm or cool a room, raise or lower a ceiling, make walls recede or advance. But all of these tricks are useless if your dislike the color itself, and so you should think about colors you *really* like best and use them to advantage.

Patterns and textures also contribute to the ambiance of a room. The very same furniture takes on a different look, depending on the fabrics and textures used with it. As we have already mentioned, classical patterns in brocades, velvets, silks, or satins will create a much grander effect than sturdier, but equally appropriate, chintz, linen, cotton, or wool. And a braided or hooked rug is much folksier than an Oriental or wall-to-wall carpeting.

Developing Your Taste

You can develop your taste and appreciation of good traditional decorating in a number of different ways. You can visit authentic restorations such as Colonial Williamsburg in Virginia, Old Sturbridge Village in Massachusetts, Winterthur in Wilmington, Delaware, the Henry Ford Museum and Greenfield Village in Dearborn, Michigan, or Shelburne Village in Vermont, to mention only a few. Your local historical society can tell you where to find restored and furnished early houses in your area. Museums offer another chance to see authentically furnished period rooms. But don't feel obliged to try to duplicate this pure authenticity; instead, look for ideas adaptable to your own use.

House tours organized for charity are another source of inspiration—either tours of private homes or "Showcase Houses," presenting each room individually done by a prominent professional decorator. Since most decorators prefer traditional styles, tours of this type offer an excellent opportunity to study their adaptation to modern living.

Start your own file of ideas. Many manufacturers of paint, wallpaper, furniture, rugs, and other products offer informative booklets, catalogs, and kits. Collect these, together with pictures, color chips, and fabric swatches that appeal to you. Play with them a little, trying out various combinations just to see how they look.

If you have the opportunity, go on the plant tours offered by many firms in the home furnishings field. (Write to the Department of Economic Development in your state capital for a list of industrial tours in your state.) Actually seeing how glass, china, silver, furniture, floor coverings, and so forth are made can help you distinguish the good from the bad or the simply mediocre.

Within the wide range of traditional American styles of decorating, you are certain to find one that is just right for you. After you have decided on the overall look you want to achieve, the rest is comparatively easy. But because each design decision you make will add to the final effect, it is important to make even your simplest choices with your overall plan in mind, always remembering that you must please yourself first—you are the final judge of the success or failure of your decorating plan.

If you love houseplants, let your green thumb show with a luxuriant display of thriving beauty in every room. Country-style furniture in this dining area is underscored by simple stenciling on the floor; shade-tolerant plants make a brave and lively showing.

CHAPTER THREE

Color in traditional decorating

Choice of colors is basic to any design scheme. Used with imagination, color can make good decorating a triumph. Used badly, it can turn the same combination of ingredients into a disaster. The difference between the two is a matter of knowing the rules of color well enough to produce harmonious relationships at whatever level of intensity you choose. Delicate or vivid, clear or shadowy, restrained to one key or modulating into several, an effective color scheme is guided by the same basic considerations. Some of these considerations have to do with the physical aspects of color; others concern its psychological effects.

Obviously, your choice of colors may also be affected by the traditions of the periods themselves, although these considerations need not restrict you.

Our Color Heritage

Color has always been a part of our heritage, but not in the abundance we know today. Our early settlers made their own dyes from natural sources. Although blues and reds were favorite colors, green, yellow, pink, and brown were also used quite frequently. Steeping the bark of walnut, chestnut, and hickory trees made brown dye; black oak and hickory bark made green. The leaves of sumac, goldenrod, laurel, and peach created varying yellows. Cochineal—prepared from the dried female bodies of a tropical American insect—made all the reds, and, when diluted, it made pink. All blues, from deepest to softest, were made from the indigo shrub, also known as anil. Anilene dyes, introduced in 1850, were originally made by distilling anil with potash, later with coal tar, and they made possible an entire new rainbow of colors.

The taste of our more affluent colonists was influenced by colors popular in England and France. During the Georgian period, colors were of medium tone, restrained and elegant—soft ivory, rose, yellow, and shades of blue and green; while in France, soft blues, gray, eggshell, or yellow prevailed. Unlike Georgian mahogany pieces, French furniture was often painted pale gray, blue, yellow, or off-white with accents of gilding or striping. During the Federal period, colors became even lighter, and many walls were painted in pastel shades.

By the turn of the eighteenth century, a dark Pompeian red, named for the new archeological find in Italy, became popular in England, along with rich shades of green, gold, and pink. During the Victorian era, walls were darker, nearly muddy shades of brown, red, or mulberry lightened by strong reds, bottle greens, and golds for drapery and upholstery fabrics. Today the range of reliable, fade-resistant colors in both textiles and paint is almost endless, and whatever your style of decorating, your choice need not be limited unless you are being completely authentic to a period.

Indigo blue, one of our oldest traditional colors, covers the sprawling contemporary sofa; a lighter version in a coordinating pattern is used to cover the two Queen Anne chairs. The floor, stenciled in the traditional manner, continues the blue-and-white scheme sparked by red.

Color and Light

If you take a little time to understand the basics of color it can work miracles for you. An important thing to know is that color is completely dependent on light. Every color we see is reflecting wavelengths of light in its own particular way, and the amount it reflects is completely dependent on the quality and intensity of the light it receives.

On a bright summer's day, nature's colors are vivid and bright, but they deepen when a storm cloud passes overhead, become still darker at twilight, and disappear completely after night falls. The colors you use in your home react in the same way to full or partial sunlight, artificial light, and no light. That is why it is so important to collect samples of any major colors you plan to use—paint, wall and floor covering, fabric—and try them at home under both day and night lighting. Because your walls and floors add the major amount of color to a room, and because color reflects upon color, intensifying the final result, your choice for these large areas will always appear much deeper in value than the samples you bring home.

Experiment with Color

Learn to use the vocabulary of color; it will help you in everything from mixing paints to analyzing color schemes you would like to copy. Experiment with the various color plans to gain confidence in selecting colors for many purposes—clothes and appetizing-looking meals as well as decorating schemes. Recognize that color changes in different kinds of light, that each color is affected by surrounding ones, and that you must experiment in order to find satisfying combinations. Above all, realize the importance of total planning—that a beautiful table setting, a flattering costume, or an attractive room is a harmonious whole and not just an unrelated assembly of parts.

Color Has Temperature

We think of color as being warm, hot, cool, cold, or passively neutral, as beige, gray, or white. Unconsciously, we associate oranges, reds, and yellows with varying degrees of sunlight or firelight; blues, greens, and violets are associated with deep forests, twilight, and cooling water; white with snow. You can use this unconscious temperature of color to warm or cool a room. Rooms facing south or southwest can be flooded with sunlight during the day; some of this hot brilliance can be absorbed with blues or greens or white. Daylight entering a room with a north or northeast exposure will be slightly blue; you can suggest the missing sunlight by using warm colors.

On the other hand, you may want to make a light, airy room even lighter and more spacious by adding to the lightness, or a dark room more intimate and cozy by darkening it even more. Whatever the exposure of a room, carefully analyze exactly how much light it does receive either directly or reflected from outside sources, such as trees or other buildings and, when choosing colors, consider the effect that any reflected colored light will have on your choices.

A complementary color scheme, such as the red and green used in this bedroom, is the boldest and most demanding on the eye. Here the scheme is softened by the predominant pink of the antique quilt on the brass bed, the white dust ruffle, and the white background of the quilt on the wall.

Color Values

The lightness or darkness of a color is referred to as its value or tone. Colors of different values affect each other when they are placed side by side. A white tone placed on a black background, for example, will appear larger than a similar tone placed on a gray background. A safe principle in decorating a traditional

Color Has a Vocabulary

At left is what is commonly called a color wheel. Some wheels contain many more colors than are shown here, usually twelve or twenty-four colors, but this one gives the basic six: yellow, green, blue, violet, red, and orange.

Hues are all colors such as yellow, red, blue, but not black, white, gray, and their mixtures.

Neutrals are black, white, gray, and grayed tones such as beige or cream.

Value refers to the lightness or darkness of a color—to light blue, dark blue, and the many gradations between.

Shades are hues with black added, making them darker in value.

Tints are hues with white added, making them lighter in value.

Intensity refers to the brightness or dullness of a color. Pure hues are the brightest and most intense.

The intensity of a hue is lowered by adding white or black or by adding some of the hue's complement. Look at this color wheel: Colors directly opposite each other on the wheel are complementary.

To gray a color, add a bit of its complement—a small amount can make the color softer, subtler. Too much can make the color very dull or cause it to lose most of its original hue.

Hundreds of colors can be made by mixing pure hues and tints and shades of hues.

Values

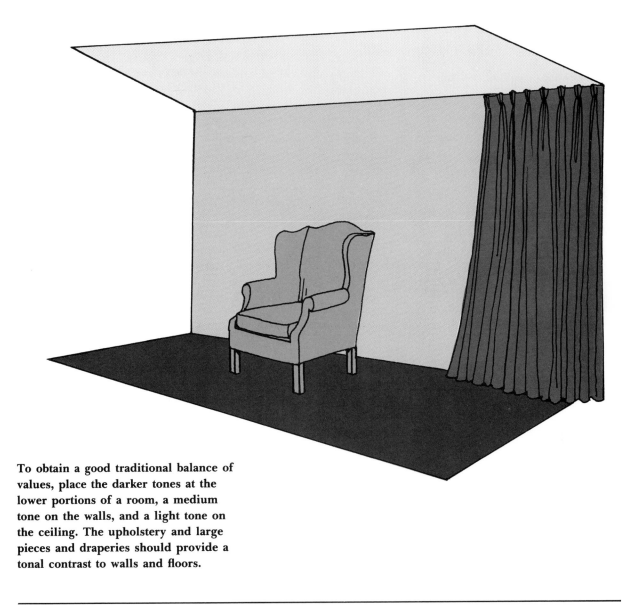

To obtain a good traditional balance of values, place the darker tones at the lower portions of a room, a medium tone on the walls, and a light tone on the ceiling. The upholstery and large pieces and draperies should provide a tonal contrast to walls and floors.

room is to place the darker tones at the lower portions of the room, a medium tone on the walls, and a light tone on the ceiling. Draperies should then provide a tonal contrast with the walls, and the upholstery should be differentiated tonally from the floors. Another point to bear in mind is that it is generally most appealing if the largest areas in a room are the most neutral. The intensity of color can be increased as the area to be covered decreases in size. However, this distribution can be altered to achieve different effects in a room, as we will see shortly.

OPPOSITE PAGE:

Light Makes a Difference

Intense colors appear brighter in strong light or sunshine. One by one the colors seem to disappear as the light fades, until finally you see only the light colors or white.

Experiment with a paint sample of a color you like:

- **Look at it in a room where you might use the color; note the effect on it of surrounding colors.**

- **Look at it on a dull day—and again when the sun is shining.**

- **Shut out the sunlight and turn on a lamp to see what happens to the color.**

- **Look at it in several locations in the room, with the light striking it from different angles.**

Artificial light often tends to change the hue as you see it. It can make a pink tablecloth appear violet or give a blue bedspread a greenish color. This is important to remember when shopping. Store lighting is different from home lighting, and home lighting varies greatly. Both are different from natural light. It's best to collect or paint the largest swatches possible that you can examine under various lighting conditions.

In a town-house living room an analogous scheme of related greens and yellows creates a serenely formal effect. Floors are stained a deep walnut; striped satin upholstery on the tub chair repeats colors in the rug. Accessories gathered from all over the world soften the room's formality, add interest of their own.

Color Can Affect Size

Perhaps as an extension of their emotional temperature, colors also have a temperamental effect. The warm ones tend to seem exciting and active, the cool ones restful and restrained. This quality of color also affects our perception of size: Tranquil colors can make a room look larger, whereas vibrant ones may seemingly shrink its dimensions because more seems to be going on.

The intensity and value of the colors used have an even greater effect on the apparent size of a room. Pale colors retreat, leading the eye into the distance. Strong, vivid colors jump out toward you. That is why a room whose walls are white or pastel seems much larger than the same-size room painted a deep or a bold color. (Still, if you prefer intense colors to pale ones, use them. Better a small room with character than a larger-looking one that seems insipid.)

You can use the eye-fooling effect of color to change the proportions of a room as well as its size. A long narrow room will look less like a hallway if you paint the short walls in a bold, advancing color. To tame an awkwardly high ceiling, paint it several shades darker than the walls; it will immediately seem to descend. White or a pale tint of the wall color will make a low ceiling look higher. An effective trick is to paint the ceiling of an entryway a very dark color, that of the adjoining living room a very light one. The contrast will make the living room seem especially large and airy.

Use a color contrasting with that of the main expanse of wall if you want to draw attention to architectural features, such as moldings, dadoes, or fireplace mantels. Conversely, if the room is too broken up by these features, or if they are ugly or undistinguished, paint them the same color as the walls and they will tend to disappear.

Basic Rules for Harmonious Color Schemes

Professional decorators usually choose one of three basic color schemes (one-color, related, or complementary) for the largest areas in a room, which include walls, floor covering, window treatments, and large upholstered pieces. The first, monochromatic, uses variations of the same color throughout. The second, analogous, uses three neighboring colors chosen from a 12-color wheel, or any three of six adjoining colors on a 24-color wheel. The third, complementary, uses two colors opposite each other on a color wheel.

A monochromatic scheme is for you if you have a strong color preference, in which case the same hue is used throughout and variety is obtained by varying the tones and intensity of the color and by using a variety of textures.

If you have no real preference, use a neutral—white, beige, or gray—livened with bright color accents such as pillows, and

This complementary use of red and green is reinforced by the combination of colors in the bright rag rug, the pink-and-green quilt on the table in the background, and the quilt-patterned pillows on the white tuxedo loveseat in the foreground.

Colors Affect One Another

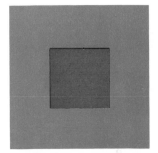

The same color can appear quite different in different surroundings, a fact to keep in mind when you are shopping. The illustrations here show what happens when orange is placed first against a yellow-green background, then against blue, and finally against lavender. Against the yellow-green, the orange looks darker, against blue it becomes more intense, and with the lavender it appears less intense.

Colors affect one another in other ways too. Some combinations sharpen the impact of each color contained in them; others make the component colors look drab, faded, or gaudy. Whenever two or more colors are to be used in a room, study them carefully to see whether they will bring out the best in each other. Just as a brown dish for scrambled eggs or a dull green one for sliced tomatoes can make these foods seem special ones, so the right color backgrounds can enhance your furnishings and accessories. In any case, it is usually most pleasing if the colors in a decorating scheme are used in unequal amounts so they don't vie with each other in importance.

other colorful accessories in either analogous or complementary colors.

If you want a warm analogous scheme you could combine values of red, orange, and yellow, or, for a cool scheme, violet, blue, and green.

Complementary schemes are the boldest and often the most interesting to the eye combining, as they do, such direct opposites as red and green or orange and blue or yellow and purple. The neutrals, white, gray, and black, are not considered additional colors in combination with complementaries, or any other color scheme for that matter, and, in fact, serve to enhance them. Also, complementaries are often more pleasing if both are mixed with a small amount of the same third color. For example, yellow and purple can be more pleasing with a little red or blue added to each.

ABOVE:

White is a dominant color in this airy living room. Vivid accents of bright colors are enhanced by their contrast to the whiteness of the room.

OPPOSITE PAGE:

A monochromatic room is created when the same hue is adopted throughout the room. Here variations on yellow tend to strengthen the warmth of the natural dark wood and the welcoming feeling of a room that might otherwise appear quite formal.

Warm and Cool Colors

Some colors appear warm—the reds, yellows, and red-violets. Others appear cool—the blues, many greens, and blue-violets. Some colors, like green, can seem either warm or cool: Yellow-greens seem warm, blue-greens seem cool. A touch of blue added to white will make it seem icy; a touch of yellow will mellow it. The intensity and value of a color also affect its apparent "temperature." Intense colors appear warmer than dull ones.

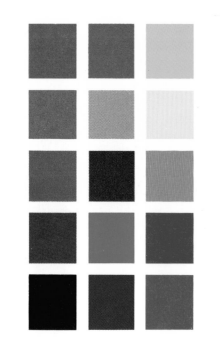

Color Can Be Too Colorful

For harmonious decorating, it's wise to make up your mind about what your major color is. New techniques and materials make possible a breathtaking range of effects undreamed of a few decades ago. Color is now imprisoned in filament yarns impervious to fading even in the strongest sunlight. Vinyl and other synthetics simulate natural materials, from leather to handwoven wool, in almost every color to be found in nature. It's easy to go overboard and use so many hues, in roughly equal amounts, that the decorating scheme lacks any one strong color note to which the others can be keyed. Even if you are only using analogous or complementary colors, do not make them of equal value or distribute them equally in a room. On the other hand, make sure that any accent color is used more than once in a room to help tie it together.

Another mistake to avoid is the use of certain colors because they are currently fashionable. Fads, and your passion for them, will pass, but you may have to live with a carpet or a major piece of furniture for some time. Be careful too about choosing colors so brilliant that you tire of them easily. This doesn't mean that you must avoid vivid colors, but only that you should use them with discretion, usually in small amounts.

Texture will also affect the colors in a room. Rough textures absorb light and thus appear darker; smooth surfaces reflect light and are therefore brighter.

Wood Is Also a Color

Too often the characteristic hues of furniture woods are ignored in planning the color scheme of a room. Yet wood takes on depth and richness when set against an appropriate background, and it loses character when it is not. Here, as elsewhere, the rules of related or contrasting color can be applied. Soft blues, blue-greens, and greens, for example, contrast with the warm tones of fine furniture and therefore flatter it. Yellow, beige, and coral are equally successful, but for the opposite reason—because they *are* related to wood tones. Grays, bright blues, and violets neither contrast with most natural wood finishes nor relate well to them, and therefore generally form an unfriendly background. Often these colors are better used with painted furniture.

Practicality is still another consideration in the choice of color, particularly if you have young children in the home. Some color-and-texture combinations—a pebbly textured rug in earth tones, for example—tend to disguise dust and dirt. Very light (or very dark) shades and smooth surfaces are more vulnerable. If you like the light, bright look, be sure to check for labels that identify soil-resistant finishes on fabrics and rugs, and opt for easily maintained hard floorings and scrubbable paints and wall coverings.

Wood is also a color—warmly glowing and patterned with its own natural grain. In this Colonial-style great room, a modern kitchen hides behind pine cabinets with porcelain knobs; dried herbs hang from rafters. Windsor chairs are used around the scrubbed-top dining table and at the hearth.

Plan for Color Harmony

There are three main methods or plans for using color, and they apply whether you are working with a table setting, an accessory grouping, or a room. Each plan can be equally good if the color values, intensities, and amounts are chosen with care. If they are not, the plan could be so intense that you could not live with it, so intense that the colors would vibrate. Or it could be so bland that it would lack impact. All three plans can incorporate neutrals.

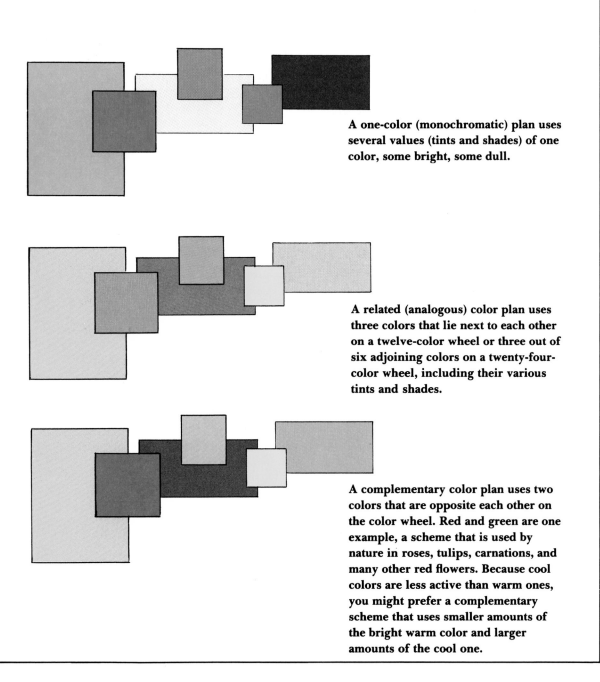

A one-color (monochromatic) plan uses several values (tints and shades) of one color, some bright, some dull.

A related (analogous) color plan uses three colors that lie next to each other on a twelve-color wheel or three out of six adjoining colors on a twenty-four-color wheel, including their various tints and shades.

A complementary color plan uses two colors that are opposite each other on the color wheel. Red and green are one example, a scheme that is used by nature in roses, tulips, carnations, and many other red flowers. Because cool colors are less active than warm ones, you might prefer a complementary scheme that uses smaller amounts of the bright warm color and larger amounts of the cool one.

Where to Find a Color Scheme

Color schemes are all around you for the borrowing. An almost inexhaustible source is to be found in patterned fabrics, carpets, and wall coverings that combine two or more colors. Begin by selecting a printed or woven pattern that appeals to you. Then match the colors that appear in it in paint chips, fabric swatches, rug and wall covering samples. (In matching colors, it is helpful to look at the original and the color you are mixing through a 1½- to 2-inch hole cut out of a sheet of white paper. When the two colors are placed next to each other and compared through the hole, the white paper isolates them from any other nearby color, making the differences between the two easily distinguishable.) Play with these by adding or subtracting colors, varying the areas in which the colors are to be used, and taking into account the basic rules of color until you are confident that the scheme you have worked out is right.

Perhaps the original pattern you selected will be used as an upholstery or slipcover fabric. The wall color might then either match the background of the print or be painted a lighter value of that color, and the print's secondary color can be borrowed for the floor covering. The brightest or strongest color in the fabric should be used for accents in the room.

Another way to get an idea of what a room will look like in color is to make several photocopies of any floor plan and elevations with windows that you may have worked out (see Chapter 5), and try out different colors and swatches on them. The large areas can be painted in for the best effect. Or you can make a chart of squares representing in relative size the ceiling, walls, floor, windows, and major pieces of furniture, and color or paste them with swatches to see how a color combination will work.

Let the Outside Come Indoors

Don't neglect the opportunity, if you are lucky enough to have a house with a view, to bring the outdoors inside. If you look out on trees, try wood-paneled walls, neutral colors in paints and floor coverings, nature's own browns and golds or greens for upholstery and curtains. Then, like nature in bloom, splash in brilliant accents of color, but in small quantities.

If an expanse of water is a major part of your view, consider its brilliance and light-reflective qualities, which tend to wash out pale or neutral colors. Build your scheme around the colors of water itself—green, blue, blue-green—with splashes of red-orange and yellow to warm it.

Whether you plan to decorate a room or a whole house from scratch or simply add something new to an existing scheme, it is important to regard your home as a unit, particularly in terms of color. Most of today's houses and apartments are open in plan, with one room clearly visible from the next. In almost any

Color Scheme

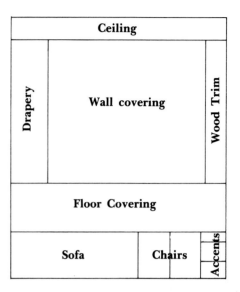

With fabric swatches and paint chips, or a set of watercolor or tempera paints, diagram the color scheme in the room. Use rectangles to represent the relative sizes of the ceiling, walls, floor, window treatments, and major furniture pieces.

Color Elevation

To visualize the arrangement of colors in a room, make several photocopies of an elevation you have drawn (see Chapter 5) and color in the areas with watercolor or tempera paint chips and fabric swatches.

For a harmonious effect, let color flow effortlessly through
adjoining rooms. Here, the same warm-color of the walls with dark-
green woodwork and moldings is echoed in both the dining room
and living room. Furniture and accessories throughout are
eighteenth-century American.

house this is true of the living and dining rooms; both are almost always in view from the front door, and so they should be compatible.

Let Color Flow Through Your House

Adjacent rooms that can be seen together should be coordinated in color, with variations in patterns and textures and in the intensity of the colors used to avoid monotony. In a unified color-flow plan, rooms can play further variations on the original color scheme, with care taken to avoid the sudden shock produced by a completely unrelated mood. For instance, the kitchen might feature fruitwood cabinets, a white painted floor, and white countertops; the accent colors could be pink, green, or yellow, all drawn from a patterned wall covering. The walls in a family room related to this kitchen might be wood-paneled, the upholstery white or yellow, with green accessories.

A color scheme of this type creates a pleasing harmony throughout the house without needless repetition of the same color. Children's rooms might sometimes be made an exception to the color-flow rule to allow for strong individual preferences. But this kind of plan is so flexible that many variations can be worked into it without destroying the overall design.

In establishing an overall color scheme, you will want to carry at least one unifying color throughout your home. Sometimes this can be done with wall-to-wall carpeting and color-related hard flooring. Another way is to make use of the many coordinated patterns available in wall coverings. For example, for an entrance hall you might choose a wallpaper pattern that repeats the color of the living room's painted walls; for the dining room and other adjacent rooms, you can select different but compatible patterns all related in color. By planning carefully in this way, you will always feel at home in any room—and so will your guests.

If you are lucky enough to have a fine view and relative privacy, leave your windows uncurtained and bring the outdoors inside. In this "garden" room, the woodwork is stained tree-trunk brown, a trellis covers a soffit painted lawn-green, and bright yellow cushions add sunlight to the room. Over the parquet-topped table hangs an accurate version of an old gas fixture.

CHAPTER FOUR

Pattern and texture

Except for color, nothing adds so much interest to a room as pattern and texture. In introducing both into your basic color scheme, you will begin to discover the endless possibilities to be found in the great variety of fabrics and floor and wall coverings available. Assembling an exciting combination of color, pattern, and texture can be as creatively satisfying as painting a picture.

Generally defined, pattern is a distinctive design that has been printed, woven, stenciled, stamped, or otherwise created on fabrics, floor coverings, and wall coverings. Pattern creates immediate visual impact and mood; texture adds a subtle third dimension of depth as well as tactile interest.

Sometimes texture is the result of pattern, as in a woven cane chair seat or a flocked wall covering, a slate, tile, or brick patterned floor, or a hooked or braided rug. Although pattern creates the initial visual impact, texture can add the subtle and ever-changing reaction of light on its surface, often lightening or darkening its apparent color.

Both pattern and texture contribute to the informal or formal look of a room. For example, we think of crewel, brocade, damask, velvet, and lace as being elegantly formal; linen, paisley, chintz, and toile are midway; and homespun, gingham, plaid, and muslin are the least formal. Stenciled patterns can span the range from formal to folksy.

Technically, everything has texture. Smooth surfaces can be very refined and elegant, but they lack the three-dimensional

OPPOSITE PAGE:

Almost any mood can be created with pattern. In this formal foyer, an intriguing geometric pattern of squares and triangles is painted on the floor to add the effect of marble. The enamelware pan and spongeware ceramic pitcher on the wall-hung console repeat forms in the painting.

A large-patterned bold wall covering will be out of scale in a small room, making it seem to be over-crowded and uncomfortably demanding on the eye.

A small wallpaper pattern can make a small room seem larger, but if it is used in a larger room, the design may be overwhelmed and loose its significance.

Color and patterns in the kitchen can be as playful as you like. Primary red and blue are used for the breakfast bar and chairs; clear green for the pass-through ledge and pantry woodwork. Cabinets surrounding a pass-through to the pantry are painted with trompe l'oeil versions of open doors and a cloudy sky glimpsed through a fanlight.

interest of rougher ones. An empty room with painted walls, a smooth floor, and an uncurtained expanse of glass at the windows is bland and dead-looking. Add a braided rug and homespun draperies, however, and the room begins to come alive in a warm, casual way.

Light is also an important factor in relation to texture. Because of reflected light, the colors in a glazed chintz pattern will appear clear and bright; colors in the same but unglazed pattern will seem to be deeper because the dull surface absorbs more light than its slick counterpart. Thus, while planning a decorating scheme, it is important to keep in mind that rough surfaces such as velvet or rugs with a deep pile will absorb more light and look darker than smooth or slick surfaces.

The rule for texture is the same as that for color and patterns. Don't overdo it. Just as a room lacking in texture is bland, so one with an excess of textured materials, or one with too many different kinds, is distracting. What is needed is a delicate balance of smooth, pile, and rough textures, each one enhancing the others.

Basic Sources of Pattern and Texture

Wall coverings. Because a wall covering is so extensive in a room, its pattern and/or texture adds considerably to the overall effect of the space. Textured wall coverings in the form

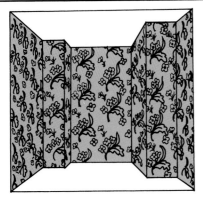

Ceiling too low? A wallpaper with a strong vertical design leads the eye upward, making the ceiling seem higher and in much better scale with the walls.

Wall pattern can also disguise unwelcome architectural defects, camouflaging jogs or patchy walls to create a unifying effect throughout the room.

If the ceiling is too high, a bold horizontal design lowers it visually improving the apparent proportions of the entire room.

of paper, cloth, or synthetic copies are available in a great variety of traditional flocked or embossed patterns plus simulations of patterns and textures ranging from the most formal damask, moiré, or marble to simple linen, ticking, brick, or fieldstone.

Wall paneling. Natural or prefinished, wall paneling is available with the texture and color of beautiful hardwood grains or of weathered barn siding; and it is also made in board-and-batten, tongue-and-groove, and other paneling forms. Natural hardwood paneling is the most expensive; pine and redwood are less costly. Since natural wood paneling must be hand-assembled, board by board, labor adds to the cost of this treatment. Look-alikes, made of hardboard with an easy-maintenance plastic surface, cost less and come in 8-foot panels for quicker and easier assembly, although many people do not find the finish as beautiful as that of natural wood.

Masonry. This category includes stone, brick, and concrete, each having a distinctive surface, which is often so three-dimensional that the play of light and shadow on it has a particularly handsome effect. A brick fireplace wall, with its variegated texture accentuated by the mortar courses, is a good example.

Paint. The least expensive covering for walls and floors is paint. In addition to just adding color, it can be patterned or textured. Some paint contains grains of silica sand that add a

This classic-looking living room exudes an atmosphere of warm formality. From the stained rafters to the flame-stitch upholstery to the finely patterned Oriental rug, a play of texture pleases the eye. Exuberant floral arrangements add a welcoming touch.

Pattern and Texture Tips

■ Like color and texture, pattern can play tricks on your eyes. A wallpaper with a vertical design, by leading the eye upward, makes a ceiling look higher, while a strong horizontal motif seemingly lowers the ceiling's height. Using wallpaper of any kind on the ceiling also makes the ceiling look lower. A large pattern may seem out of scale in a small room, a small pattern in a large room tends to be overwhelmed. A great deal of pattern in a room seems to fill it up, reducing the need for furniture; in a large room that can be an advantage, but in a small room the space may seem crowded.

■ Pattern can disguise architectural defects. In a hall or foyer cut up by many doors, the walls *and* doors can be covered with an exciting pattern to give it a unified—and interesting—look. A small allover pattern is good for disguising uneven walls, jogs, and other blemishes.

■ Using a patterned fabric on draperies and on one or more large upholstered or slipcovered pieces often helps to tie a room together. If the fabric is chintz, one chintz pattern is usually sufficient for any room.

continued on next page

stuccolike texture to a wall—you simply roll or brush it on. Or you can add pattern to wet paint by dabbing it with a sponge, stippling it with a brush made especially for that purpose, or running a heavy comb across the wet surface in any pattern you might like—swirling, cross-hatch, horizontal, or vertical stripes to mention a few. You can even gain a two-color pattern *and* texture by applying a base coat of one color, letting it dry completely, and then adding a thicker paint of another color to be sponged, stippled, or combed, so that the undercoat color shows through. Paint dealers supply the special thicker paint and necessary tools.

Any of these techniques should be practiced on a wide board before they are attempted on your walls or ceilings. Be certain that you really like the textured effect because, once applied, it is difficult to revert to a smooth surface.

Textiles. An almost unlimited variety of patterns and textures are available in textiles. In fact, texture in fabric is defined as the character and arrangement of threads in a woven pattern. The character of the spun thread—smooth, nubby, or fuzzy—contributes as much to the final texture as does the manner of weaving—tight and close, loose, or somewhere in between.

Natural fibers include linen, cotton, silk, and wool. Linen is woven in various textures from the sheerest gauze to the heaviest basketweave. Cotton spans a wide range from silky percale to rough homespun, velvet, and corduroy. Silk is used to create the most luxurious velvets, brocades, damasks, moirés, and satins. Wool is sometimes used for fine-textured upholstery fabrics or window curtains, but it's used more frequently for rugs or carpets with textures that vary from single-level loop to sculptured or shaggy.

Synthetic fibers, used alone or in combination, such as a cotton and Dacron combination, cost less than natural ones and can be woven or spun to create a facsimile of any natural fiber fabric. Most often they are fade- and soil-resistant and have little or no shrinkage.

Rosemaling

For the past several centuries, European folk art painting has brightened furniture, walls, and accessories of various types—mirrors, boxes, trays, canisters—with exuberant pattern and vivid color. Emigrants from each country brought their particular ethnic version of folk art design to our land. While there is a certain naive kinship among folk art painting from all European countries, perhaps the most highly developed and sophisticated technique, called rosemaling, evolved in Scandinavia during the early part of the eighteenth century.

Literally translated, rosemaling means "rose painting," but the art form has expanded to include other flower forms as well as fruits and an occasional human or animal figure. If you have even a small talent for drawing you might want to try your hand at this venerable craft. Three basic brush-stroke shapes—a circle, an S, and a C—are used to create beautifully flowing patterns that can be as simple or as sophisticated as you like.

Stenciled Patterns

Since the beginning of our country, stenciling has played an important part in adding distinctive decoration to floors, walls, furniture, and fabrics in homes of all types, from the simplest to the most elegant.

Wealthier colonists chose their stencil patterns from designs that were carried from town to town by itinerant craftsmen who stayed on in a house and received room and board while applying their craft. Simpler householders made their own stencil patterns, often based on those they had seen in wealthier homes.

Stenciling also decorated our earliest rugs that were made of sailcloth. Known as painted floor cloths, these rugs were extremely popular from the first quarter through the middle of the eighteenth century, when wealthier colonists turned to rugs and carpets imported from England. With today's overwhelming interest in traditional American decorating, floor cloths are becoming increasingly popular as small accent rugs.

Creating your own stencil patterns. An authentic and inexpensive design can be added to almost any surface with the easy-to-master technique of stenciling. Art-supply stores offer stencil kits with all the equipment needed, including instructions, as well as individual stenciling supplies if you prefer to create your own designs.

In all stenciling the cutout pattern must be firmly and flatly attached to the surface to be decorated. Then special stencil paints are applied with stencil brushes in a rapid, vertical dabbing motion, rather than with the usual flat brush stroke. The paint must always be of the right consistency—neither too thin to run, nor too thick to build up.

If you start from scratch you will need stiff and transluscent stencil paper, a small, sharp razor-blade knife, blunt stencil brushes, small containers for mixing paints, fast-drying Japan paint for hard surfaces or textile paint for fabrics, a thinner for each type of paint, and a supply of clean rags.

To cut the stencil pattern, trace the design on the stencil paper, place the paper over a piece of glass, and cut out elements with the knife. If you plan to use more than one color in your design, cut a separate stencil for each.

Stenciling a floor or wall. First scrub the surface to remove any traces of wax or grease before applying a base coat of paint in the color of your choice. After the base coat is thoroughly dry, use a chalk line to lay out a grid of guidelines for the repeat of

■ Generally speaking, if you have a rug or carpet with a bold design or a strongly-patterned wall covering, subdue the patterns in window and upholstery fabrics. If in doubt, simplify your decision by choosing from among the large selection of coordinated fabrics and wall coverings offered by many large manufacturers. The same rule applies to texture. One strong pattern and one strong texture are usually enough in any room. However, patterns of the same scale can often be combined successfully, particularly if they are related in color; and, if skillfully balanced by plain surfaces, patterned or Oriental rugs may be used with printed fabrics.

■ A bold, strongly colored, or splashy pattern is usually better confined to a fairly small or infrequently used area, such as an entry hall or bathroom, where it will provide a center of interest and will not be looked at long enough to become disturbing. Used too lavishly, such patterns will soon seem to be overpowering.

■ Two or more patterns can be pleasing if they are related in color and mood. For example, you can use a bold plaid with a stripe or with a small floral, or a traditional flame stitch with a small floral or geometric, or a bold chintz with a small plaid or sprigged floral.

For the past few centuries, immigrants have brought with them their knowledge of European folk art painting to decorate furniture, walls, and accessories of various types. This particular type of decoration, called rosemaling, evolved in Scandinavia during the early part of the eighteenth century and is, perhaps, the most exuberant of all forms of folk art.

OPPOSITE PAGE:

In a sparsely furnished Colonial-style bedroom, white-cotton bed curtains and canopy are of muslin stenciled with an authentic pattern. With a little practice, stenciling is an easy way to add distinctive pattern and color to floors, walls, and fabrics.

your pattern. Follow the grid while stenciling your pattern, moving it from one area to the next. Protect your work, after it is thoroughly dry, with two or three coats of polyurethane.

Stenciling fabrics. Start with white or light-colored cotton or linen, which is best for stenciling. Wash the fabric thoroughly to remove any sizing, and then press it to remove wrinkles. Use pushpins or masking tape to stretch the fabric tightly over a working surface covered with white blotting paper. Use color-fast textile paint to apply the pattern, and let it dry for twenty-four hours. To set the colors, place a clean dry cloth over the design and press slowly with a warm iron. Repeat several times on both sides of the fabric.

To stencil a floor cloth you can use sailcloth—as our ancestors did—if you have ready access to a ship's supply yard, or you can substitute artist's canvas, which is more readily available at art-supply stores and equally appropriate. Stitch a one-inch hem around the edges of the cloth. Then tack or tape it down on a protected surface and paint on the background color, using an acrylic paint. After the background has thoroughly dried, follow the stenciling procedure described for floors.

OPPOSITE PAGE:

You can be as daring as you like in your choice of stencil patterns. This unusual floor is stenciled with designs taken from old sugar and flour sacks. Original stencils of this type, usually of metal, can sometimes be found in antiques shops.

Structural elements can be emphasized to create dramatic pattern. In this story-and-a-half living room, walnut-stained ceiling beams are in sharp contrast to white walls. A wall-hung quilt, table cover, and Oriental rugs add texture and bright pattern.

BELOW:

Pattern can also be cozy and enveloping. Blue-and-white sheets are used to cover the walls (see Chapter 7), to make tab window curtains, and to surround the bed. The pillow shams and quilted comforter, in a coordinated pattern, and the old quilt add texture and bright color.

Spatter Patterns for a Floor

For an informal early American look, spattering with little drops of paint is the easiest way to add pattern and color to a floor, and you can use whatever colors you like—a background color plus two to five more for the spatter pattern.

Begin by painting a thoroughly clean and dry floor with deck paint. After the background color is completely dry, dip a wisk broom in acrylic paint of a contrasting color, hold it right side up above the floor, and tap it sharply at the base to release droplets of paint. If you use more than one spatter color, you will need to wash the whisk broom before changing to the next color. Again, it is best to practice the spatter technique on a piece of paper before trying it on a floor. Fine droplets work best with some space between them, and let each color dry before moving on to the next.

After the spatter pattern is completely dry, protect it with at least two coats of polyurethane varnish.

Like stenciling, the spatter technique is designed to recreate the handmade quality in your floor designs. It takes only a little practice to achieve a very skillful effect, and the final results are rewarding.

Stencil Tips

■ **Practice on a scrap of wood or a piece of cloth until you master the technique.**

■ **Remember to keep the paint thinned to the right consistency required for clean lines.**

■ **Always dab paint vertically from directly over the surface.**

■ **After applying paint, lift the pattern carefully to avoid smearing and wipe off any remaining traces of paint on the stencil before moving on to the next section.**

■ **If the design has more than one color, you can save time by using a separate brush for each.**

CHAPTER FIVE

Planning your rooms

In every room, furniture should be arranged for convenience, for balance, and for an unimpeded flow of traffic into, through, and out of the room. There are two ways of achieving this. You can move everything about until you are exhausted, or you can measure the room and the furniture you have or hope to put in it and plan an arrangement on grid paper first. The latter method is a great saver of time and temper. If resorted to before you even buy the furniture, it can produce the best results of all.

First Considerations

In order to plan successfully you need to analyze the way you live, how you entertain, and the amount of space you have to work with. If you have a separate dining room, for instance, what size table will it accommodate and how many guests can it seat? Perhaps, as is often the case in new houses and most apartments, a part of the living room is your dining area. A drop-leaf table in an area like this can save living space and double as a buffet for larger parties.

Ideally speaking, the furniture in any room should also be arranged to achieve an eye-pleasing balance in scale, pattern, color, and texture. Balancing the visual weight of the various objects in a room makes the space attractive and inviting rather than simply functional. Height is also important. Avoid the

OPPOSITE PAGE:

In this bower of a bedroom, a cater-cornered arrangement of the bed frees wall space for storage units and for a comfortable easy chair. The tall screen breaks up the monotony of a room full of furniture at the same height.

Questions to Ask When Planning a Room

- **When planning the general living areas, ask yourself, how do you prefer to entertain and how frequently?**

- **Do you entertain guests in more than one area of the home?**

- **Where and how do you relax?**

- **Do other members of your family entertain? Where?**

- **Do you need one space for entertaining and another for relaxing?**

- **Do you or others in your family have any hobbies?**

- **Can the hobbies be stored, or must they be left out in the room?**

- **When planning the cooking and eating areas, ask yourself, what kinds of meals do you eat at home and how frequently?**

- **How many people eat together?**

- **Do your meals and your entertaining require extensive or minimal food preparation?**

- **Where do you prefer to eat?**

- **Do you cook anywhere other than in the kitchen?**

- **Do you do any food preservation and how much?**

- **Do you need extra space for storing food?**

- **Do you require special appliances and food-serving equipment?**

- **When planning a bedroom, ask yourself, what activities—such as sewing or studying—are done in the room?**

- **Does the bedroom have space for more furniture than a bed? If so, how large should each additional piece be?**

- **How much storage do you require?**

monotony of a roomful of furniture that is all at the same level by including a high-backed chair, a tall bookcase, or breakfront, a folding screen, or even a sizable mirror hanging on a wall where it will also reflect light and increase the apparent size of a room. Additional relief can be achieved with floor-to-ceiling window treatments.

To maximize the use and look of the walls in a room, it is often helpful to measure the walls and the objects that would be placed against them and sketch each wall out on grid paper. This type of plan, called an elevation, can save you many headaches.

Plan around a focal point in the room, a single major point of emphasis, such as a view, as a welcoming feature, and a series of minor points of emphasis to lead the eye into and around the room.

Traffic and Mobility

A few rules about traffic and mobility in a room should always be kept in mind. First, arrange furniture to allow for an easy flow of traffic into and throughout a room. The recommended width for major traffic clearances is four to five feet. Walk into the room in the manner and direction normally taken by the family. Make note of the clearances required to prevent obstruction of furniture in that path. In a living room, study, or family room, allow ample legroom between sofa and coffee table; fifteen inches between coffee table and chair or sofa is standard. End tables should be approximately level with the arm of a sofa for ease in reaching a cup, glass, book, or anything else on the tabletop. The height of a coffee table is really a matter of preference; some are adjustable. It goes without saying that any table should be in scale with its use and relationship to the other pieces in a room. A tiny table would look absurd beside a massive chair or topped with an oversized lamp. Good lights for reading should be placed on tables next to the most comfortable chairs.

In general, allow a minimum of 30 inches for passage between two pieces of furniture, or between a piece of furniture and a wall, but add several extra inches for a busy kitchen thoroughfare. A chest, buffet, or similar item with drawers requires a clearance of at least 36 inches. The clearance behind a chair or stool at a dining table or counter should be at least 30 inches, or 50 inches if the space behind the seat also serves as a passageway.

Floor Plans

The easiest way to arrive at a workable furniture arrangement is to make an accurate floor plan of the room in question on ¼-inch graph paper, giving each square the value of one foot. To

Elevations

Added to the floor plan, an elevation gives you a clear idea of how the complete room will look. Simply measure the walls and all furnishings on or against them, sketching their shapes on grid paper (a scale of ¼-inch to an inch is preferable).

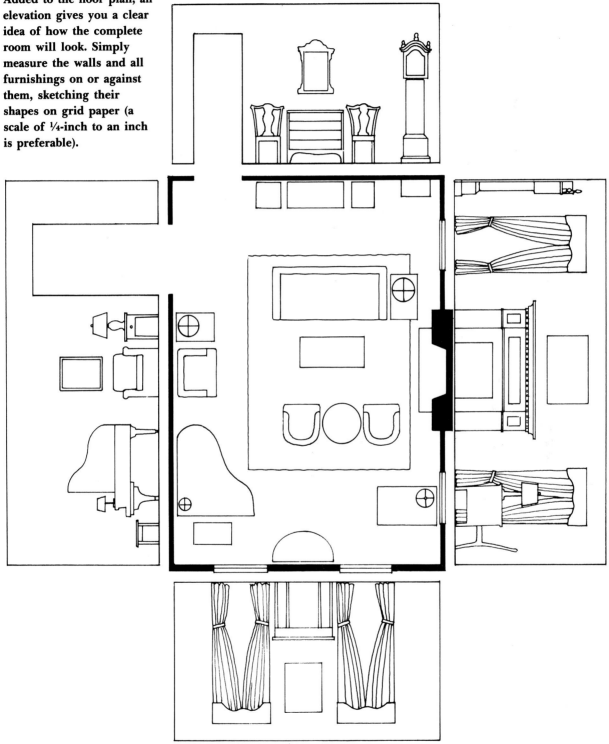

Colonial simplicity in room arrangement is exemplified in this serene dining room. At the center of the room, framed by a handsome Oriental rug, the scrubbed and waxed drop-leaf table is surrounded by hoop-back Windsor chairs and lighted by a many-armed chandelier. Extra chairs against the wall, ready for larger parties, flank an antique cabinet that provides handy storage. The hand-painted mural above the dado depicts the house and surrounding landscape, including family pets, and adds very personal interest.

Traffic Patterns

Furniture should be arranged for an unimpeded flow of traffic into, through, and out of the room. Include doorways in your planning.

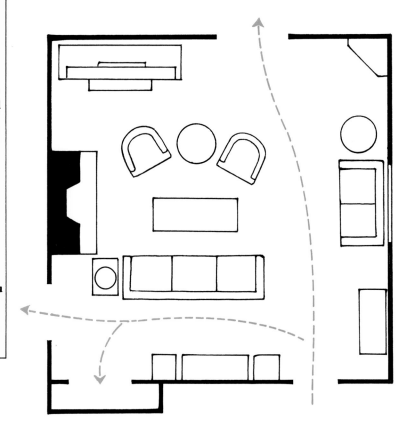

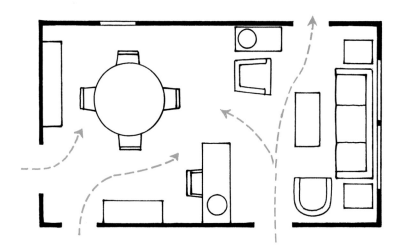

measure the room, you will need a six-foot folding wooden rule, which is more accurate than a metal tape measure, and a 12-inch ruler for marking the dimensions on your plan. Begin by measuring each wall from one corner to the next to obtain the overall size; then go back and measure the width and exact wall location of all windows, doorways, built-ins, closets—anything that interrupts wall space—and mark the size and location on your floor plan. Also show the position of electrical and telephone outlets. This will give you a clear picture of the amount of wall space you have to work with, as well as an indication of likely traffic lanes throughout the room.

Next make a list of the furniture you plan to use and measure the width, length, and height of each, jotting down the dimensions on your list as you go along. You can then use graph paper to make a pattern for each piece, or if the templates provided at the back of this book conform to the size of your furniture use them as patterns for working out your floor plans. Cut the patterns out, trace them on cardboard, then cut out the cardboard templates marking the dimensions of the corresponding piece of furniture on each. You can now use the templates on your paper floor plan, moving them about until you find the arrangement that works best.

Planning the Living and Dining Areas

It is best to determine the placement of the largest pieces of furniture first because they require more space. The most effective placement for a sofa is parallel to a wall (either against it or out from the wall about parallel to it) or at right angles to the wall.

A natural focal point, such as a fireplace or a large window with a beautiful view, can be dramatized by arranging your major pieces of furniture around it—a sofa facing the focal point and larger chairs or loveseats at right angles to the sofa. Or, if you have matching sofas, they can flank the focal point. If

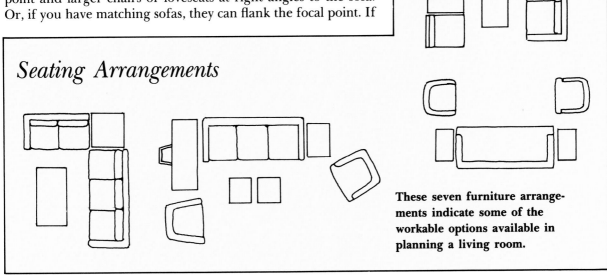

These seven furniture arrangements indicate some of the workable options available in planning a living room.

Seating Arrangements

Dining Room Plan

In planning a dining room, allow a minimum of 32 inches behind each chair, or 36 inches for a passageway behind the diner. Allow 20 inches for each diner.

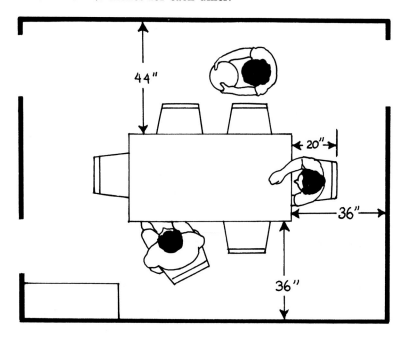

the room lacks a focal point, you can create one with an important arrangement of pictures or a large screen on the wall, either behind or facing the sofa. Always keep the proportions of your room in mind. Generally speaking, a sofa placed against the longest wall and flanked by two chairs is the nucleus of a living-room arrangement. Coffee and lamp tables will fall into place once the position of the sofa is established.

If a room is long and narrow, try breaking up its shape with furniture that juts out into the room, or you can divide the length by using one end of the room for reading, music, or television and the other for general conversation. If a room is very small, you have no choice but to arrange the furniture around its perimeter. In a very large room, more than one comfortable grouping is possible, but to assure easy conversation, avoid scattering pieces too far apart.

After you have hit upon a comfortable and convenient arrangement, check it for balance of scale, color, and texture. Color in the outlines on the floor plan to make the effect as accurate as possible.

The height dimensions won't show on the plan, but as already mentioned, it's important to include them in your calculations, and drawing elevations of the walls can also be quite helpful.

If your house has an open plan, or if, as is almost always the case, one room is visible from another, take care to plan the whole area together so that there will be a harmonious flow of design as far as the eye can see.

OPPOSITE PAGE:

A massive fireplace made of fieldstone creates a bold texture and a natural pattern that are carefully balanced by the colorful drapery and upholstery fabric and delicately textured rug.

Good planning in the dining area of this multipurpose family kitchen leaves space for a comfortable banquette, allows ample room for each diner and a wide enough path to carry a serving dish around the table. A work and storage island forms a visual barrier between the open kitchen and dining area.

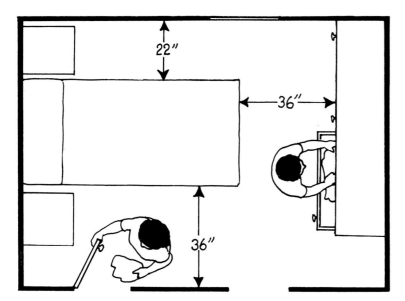

Bedroom Plan

For moving about comfortably in a bedroom allow at least 22 inches between wall and bed for making the bed and 36 inches of clearance for opening a chest of drawers or a closet door. If the room is very small and sleeps two, consider a space-saving arrangement of twin beds placed at right angles.

Planning a Bedroom

Bedrooms can also be planned on paper by making cutouts the size of the bed(s) and of movable storage units—chests, dressers, bookcases—as well as bedside tables and any chairs. You may find that placing the headboard of a large bed across a corner works better than placing it against a wall: The wall space thus released might better accommodate the storage units, and it may be easier to move freely around the bed. Also pay attention to the space needed for opening drawers and doors.

Planning the Kitchen

Because planning a kitchen presents special problems, kitchens are treated separately in Chapter 12. Today, as in the very first days of this country, the kitchen tends to be the heart of the home, and almost every kitchen, unless it's very small, can be made to serve more than one purpose by the judicious choice and arrangement of furniture, some of it built in. This purely functional area can be made into a friendly, inviting room where even the cook lingers after work is done.

One last word of advice: Play the floor-plan game whenever you want to give a room a new look, not just when you're considering major changes. This will often show you how the addition (or sometimes the elimination) of a few pieces or the rearrangement of existing ones can improve the room's balance, flexibility, and drama.

CHAPTER SIX

Floors and floor coverings

Next to the visual expanse of the room's four walls, the major area in the decoration of any room is the floor. Both the basic flooring material itself and any covering you might use on it will contribute considerably to the final decorative effect of the entire space.

The basic flooring material may be natural or man-made and, because of today's advanced technology, natural flooring can be simulated to an astonishing extent. Natural materials are usually more difficult and expensive to install and, unless you are building or remodeling, synthetics can often give you the same look for less money.

Natural Flooring Materials

This category of flooring includes wood, ceramics, marble, and concrete. Wood is the warmest and most comfortable underfoot, which is one of its greatest attributes. The harder surfaces wear well, but they are noisier and much harder on the feet.

Natural wood flooring. Both hard and soft woods are used to make natural wood flooring. Hardwood comes from deciduous trees, such as oak, walnut, or maple; soft from pine, spruce, and fir. Board widths used for flooring vary from very narrow to wide planks. The strip method of laying floors is the most

OPPOSITE PAGE:

A floor of brick, flagstone, or slate creates an informal country look while adding interesting pattern. Except in new construction or extensive remodeling, installation of the real thing is difficult, but a similar effect can be obtained with man-made look-alikes. Real brick is hard underfoot, but it is extremely easy to care for and beautiful to look at.

In this informal living room one traditional stencil pattern is used across the floor and another forms a border, eliminating the need for rugs. A camelback sofa, a comb-backed Windsor, and Boston rocking chairs surround the simple table. Staffordshire figures and salt-glaze jugs decorate the mantel.

common, with 2½-inch wide boards, usually of oak, all running in the same direction.

Parquet. Patterned hardwood flooring, usually surrounded with a border, is known as parquet. It is made from narrow strips of one or more natural woods joined so that the grain alternates to form herringbone, block, checkered, and other patterns. Preformed parquet is made in 12-inch-by-12-inch squares for easier installation.

New wooden flooring should be sealed with varnish to prevent stains from penetrating its porous surface. All types of wooden flooring, old or new, can be stained to deepen their natural color, or they can be sanded and bleached and then stained almost any color you might want, while still retaining their natural wood grain. Or you may prefer to paint an old floor a solid color, using deck paint or enamel, and then adding a stencil or spatter pattern. (See the stencil and spatter pattern sections in Chapter 4.)

Marble. Once considered a luxury, marble is now available in a thin gauge that is affordable and relatively easy to install. Marble is especially suitable for small areas, such as a foyer or bathroom, but even for a living or dining room, it can be very effective and often eliminates the need for a rug or carpet. Marble comes in marvelous colors and may be used to achieve either a formal or informal effect. It needs only an occasional washing (but never with an acid cleaner) to maintain its pristine and somewhat cold appearance. Oil will stain it, however.

Flagstone, slate, and brick. An informal or country look can be produced with flagstone, slate, and brick. The textural effect is pleasant and the care required is minimal, but, of course, these materials are a bit hard and cold on the feet. Flagstone should be sealed with a water-based or varnish sealer. Slate scratches can be concealed with a four-to-one mixture of turpentine to boiled linseed oil.

Terra-cotta and ceramic-glazed tile. Both of these types of tiles have a long history of use, particularly in countries bordering the Mediterranean and in the Middle East. Unglazed terra-cotta quarry tiles—which must be sealed before use—come in natural earth tones in different shapes and are used in informal settings. More formal effects can be achieved with glazed and ornamented ceramic tiles, which are available in a wide variety of shapes, colors, and patterns. These tiles require neither sealing nor polishing. They are particularly well suited for use on walls and counters in kitchens and bathrooms, and they require no maintenance other than washing.

Concrete. After it has been sanded, buffed, sealed, and waxed, concrete makes an admirable flooring material, especially for basement and outdoor areas. It is possible to add color to the concrete mix before it is put down, and the surface can be softened with the addition of a rug.

Terra-cotta quarry tiles are natural complements to the brick-faced walls and combination work center/eating island in this kitchen. Quarry tiles are extremely durable and relatively easy to maintain, but they are cold and hard underfoot.

Man-made Hard-Surface Flooring

In addition to those hard-surface floorings that simulate natural flooring materials, manufacturers offer an enormous variety of patterns, colors, and textures in either sheet or individual tile form and in a number of different materials that are described below.

Sheet vinyl. Sheet vinyl is stocked in rolls of 6-, 9-, and 12-foot widths that reduce or even eliminate the need for seams, if the size of a room coincides with one of the standard sheet widths. Inlaid sheet vinyl is the most expensive type, but it is well worth the extra money in wear. This is a solid vinyl in which the colors and pattern go all the way through to the backing. Rotogravure sheet vinyl patterns are photographed and printed on the surface of the vinyl and protected from wear by layers of clear vinyl or polyurethane; the thickness of the wear layers ranges from 10 to 25 mils—the thicker the layer, the longer the wear.

Some sheet vinyls are also cushioned with a backing of spongy foam to add extra resilience, making them quieter and more comfortable to walk on, as well as adding a degree of insulation. All sheet vinyls, particularly the heavier inlaid type, are more difficult for amateurs to install than the less cumbersome tiles. Vinyl, whether in sheet or tile form, is hard-wearing, easy to clean, waterproof, and resistant to most domestic spills.

Solid vinyl tiles. Like sheet vinyl, solid vinyl tiles are expensive and offer superior wearability. They are made in direct imitation of natural flooring materials and are also available in a rainbow of colors and a variety of patterns. Many of them have their own built-in adhesive—you simply pull off a protective backing and press each tile in place.

Vinyl-coated cork tiles. These tiles offer the natural beauty of real cork, sealed by a protective coating of vinyl, as well as providing quiet comfort underfoot and easy maintenance.

Vinyl asbestos tile. Less expensive than the solid vinyl, vinyl asbestos tile resists stains and wears well, but it is more brittle and less quiet underfoot and must be heated before it is laid in place.

Rubber tile. Although rubber tile is comfortable, quiet, and hard-wearing, it is also expensive and requires more waxing maintenance to retain its colorful appearance. It is sold in sheet and tile forms, with a smooth or textured surface. Some texture is recommended for safe tractability.

Asphalt tile. This material is less expensive than the other tiles, but it is also susceptible to dents and stains and is noisier underfoot.

Some hard-surface floor coverings are made with a no-wax finish; others require waxing to maintain a satisfactory appearance. Whatever your choice, be sure to follow the manufacturer's directions for cleaning and maintenance.

Wall-to-wall carpeting is particularly desirable in a bedroom for its luxurious feel underfoot, as well as its easy maintenance. Area rugs are sometimes placed over wall-to-wall carpeting to add interest (this one leads the eye to the sitting area) and to protect the carpeting in major traffic areas.

Almost all man-made flooring can be installed over an old floor if it is smooth and sound; if it is not, cushioned vinyl will often absorb the imperfections of an old floor. It may be necessary, however, to lay a subfloor of plywood sheets or particle board to create a smooth surface for your new installation.

Another consideration is where you plan to use the flooring; a basement room is called below-grade, a ground-floor room without a basement is called on-grade. Some man-made flooring cannot tolerate the moisture problems in these areas, so check with your dealer to be certain that your choice of flooring can be used for the room you have in mind. Some sheet vinyls can be used below- or on-grade or in moisture-prone kitchens and bathrooms. Solid vinyl, vinyl asbestos, asphalt, and rubber tiles can be used on any floor.

Soft-Surface Flooring

When you shop for soft-surface floor coverings—as rugs and carpets are called in the trade—choose with care and take samples of the colors and patterns in a room with you. The color, pattern, and texture will be key factors in your final scheme. But practicality—not only wearability but also which type will work best for you—should also be considered when deciding between rugs and carpets.

Wall-to-wall carpet. Because wall-to-wall carpeting is permanently installed, it is a major and often long-term investment. If you move you *can* take it with you, but there is always the expense of labor and some waste of yardage involved in removing carpet. Although it must be cleaned on location, wall-to-wall offers the advantage of one-step maintenance, as opposed to the combination cleaning of rugs and bare floors. It also creates an unbroken expanse of color and/or pattern, which has the effect of enlarging a room. And it is very comfortable underfoot, which makes it particularly desirable in a bedroom. Carpet is available in broadloom widths of 9, 12, 15, or 18 feet, the most common being 12 and 15. The term *broadloom* refers to the width of the loom on which the carpet is made and is not an indication of quality.

When shopping for carpeting, it is wise to take home a sample, if possible, to look at under both daylight and artificial light in the room where it will be used. This way you can be more sure that the color is right.

Rugs. Whether room-size or area-size, rugs can be rolled up for moving or for a trip to the cleaners. They can also be repositioned to equalize the wear of traffic patterns, whereas wall-to-wall installations are fixed. Rugs may define an area of a room or accent the floor with color and design, and they are particularly desirable in homes that have attractive wood floors to show off. Small rugs are often used over carpeting to accent an area or to reduce wear in a heavily trafficked spot.

To provide a light foil for the dark furniture in this bedroom, the floor was painted white. The neutral straw rug defines the area around the bed that is placed away from the wall to gain full advantage of the fireplace. A vertically striped wall covering adds visual height to the room; the striped look is cleverly continued by the bedcovers.

Room-size rugs. If you want a wall-to-wall effect with all the advantages of a rug, order a room-size rug that will cover your floor from baseboard to baseboard, or within about a foot of the baseboard, as desired. If you prefer a wall-to-wall look and the length of your room is within one of the broadloom widths, you will be able to have a luxurious carpet without any seams.

Indoor-outdoor carpet. As its name implies, this carpet can be used indoors or out. Particularly useful in kitchens and bathrooms or outdoors on a deck or patio, it is made of polypropylene or solution-dyed acrylic with a special moisture-proof backing to protect it against indoor spills and outdoor weather. It is also inexpensive to replace.

Planning for Rugs and Carpets

Before shopping for a rug or a carpet, first decide whether the floor covering is to become part of the background or a center of interest. Is the room formal or informal? What color should it be? Consider the color: A room with a lot of natural light may be more comfortable with cool greens and blues; cool north rooms may need warm reds, golds, and oranges. Dark rooms may seem lighter with the addition of tints of either warm or cool colors.

Also consider the size of the room. Light, cool colors in carpets or rugs will blend with the wood of the surrounding floor to make the room appear larger; deep, warm colors and dark colors may make the room appear smaller.

What other colors are in the room? Light-colored carpets will silhouette darker furniture, and vice versa. Tints and shades of the chosen colors in your furniture and window treatments may add interest to the color scheme and unify it. A rug that is varicolored or of a single dashing hue can give life to a neutral color scheme. One with a strong pattern can set the color scheme for an entire room. A rug or a carpet in a medium shade of a solid color usually becomes part of the background of the room. It can tame a bright, busy room and visually enlarge the space.

Practically speaking, white or pale tints and very dark shades of any color will show soil the most; medium color values and two-tone mixtures will show the least. Allover patterns are also practical. The same color-practicality rules apply to how traffic lanes will affect your carpet. A dense, low pile in a strong color or pattern will be the least affected by traffic; a shag will not hold up as well.

Carpet Construction

When we speak of carpet construction we refer to three factors: the method by which it is constructed, the backing on which it is constructed, and the way in which it is dyed.

OPPOSITE PAGE:

A beautifully patterned, large rug makes a strong statement in an otherwise delicately decorated bedroom, while providing soft comfort underfoot. It also echoes the pink and green of the bedcovers and other accessories, thereby helping to unify the room.

The four primary methods of carpet construction are woven, tufted, needlepunched, and knitted. A fifth method—bonded—is used in only a small percentage of today's carpeting. Although carpets of high quality may be produced by any method described here, some methods are more versatile than others.*

Woven. Weaving, by which the pile yarns and the backing yarns are interwoven simultaneously, is the original carpet construction. The three most common weaves—velvet, Wilton, and Axminster—differ in the number of pile yarns and the complexity of the loom used, as well as in the design possibilities of each.

Velvet weave, the simplest of all, is made with uniform pile that can be cut, twisted, or left in loop form. It is available in many solid colors or in tweeds.

Wilton carpeting can be made with cut or uncut pile or with multi-level loops, but normally only five colors can be used on the loom at once. Therefore, most of these carpets are made in solid colors.

Axminster is the most versatile weave in terms of color and pattern, and can be woven in endless variety because each tuft is inserted individually from a different spool of yarn. The pile is cut, but it can be long or short and have a number of different textures from smooth to pebbly.

Tufted. The tufted method, which is the fastest and therefore the most economical, is used in approximately 90 percent of the carpets and rugs manufactured today. In tufting, a large multiple-needle machine inserts tufts of yarn into a prefabricated backing which is then covered on the underside with a heavy latex coating that holds the tufts in place. A secondary backing is added for extra strength.

Needle-punched. The original felted type of indoor-outdoor carpet was needle-punched. For its construction, a webbing of short fibers is mechanically held together by the action of felting needles that interlock the fibers. For outdoor use the back is then coated with latex or another weather-resistant material. Sponge or foam backing is added for indoor use. This carpeting is not recommended for use on wood surfaces exposed to weather.

Knitted. Only a small percentage of carpets are knitted. In knitted carpets, the pile yarns are interlooped with backing yarns, and a coating of latex is applied to the backing. With this method of construction design possibilities are limited.

Bonded. Commercial carpets are frequently made using this method, and there is good reason to believe that this process will become more common. In bonding, the yarns are placed upright and bonded to both the backing and a reinforcement layer in a single operation.

*The information presented in this section appears in the pamphlet, *The Selection and Care of Rugs and Carpets* by Constance C. Adams and Regina Rector, published by the Cooperative Extension Services of the Northeast States.

Carpet Backing

The backing of a carpet should be firm and strong enough to increase the carpet's stability. A so-called *primary backing*, the material into which the yarn is placed, is usually made from jute or polypropylene. A *secondary backing*, usually made of jute, waffle-embossed rubber, latex, foam, or polypropylene, is premanufactured and glued to the primary backing of all tufted carpets and occasionally to other carpets. Check the carpet label for suggested use.

Dyeing and Printing

Carpets and rugs are dyed or colored in one of four ways: By solution dyeing, yarn dyeing, piece dyeing, or printing.

Solution dyeing. In this method, which is especially resistant to fading, dyes are added to fiber solutions before the fibers are spun.

Carpet Type	Characteristics
SINGLE-LEVEL-LOOP	Tightly woven looped carpet; least affected by traffic; very strong, especially if the loops are short; withstands water and stains; wears well on stairs.
HIGH-AND-LOW-LOOP	Variegated texture with a sculptured effect; very durable; wears well on stairs.
TWIST	An irregular and durable surface of uncut loops made with heat-set twisted yarns. Wears well on traffic areas.
RANDOM-SHEARED	Pile with sheared high strands and low level loops that give a sculptured effect; if the pile is not thick, the pattern may flatten out; durable for high-traffic areas; wears well on stairs.
TIP-SHEARED	Mixture of loops and cut pile; unlike random-sheared, the pile is cut on the same level as the loops to resist traffic.
PLUSH VELVET	Evenly cut, generally dense pile that resists crushing and bending, but tends to show footprints and soil more than others. The thicker the pile, the less shading from traffic.
SHAG	Comes in varying yarn lengths, from ¾ up to two inches long that give a grasslike appearance. Yarn may be looped or cut. Tends to mat in high-traffic areas.

Yarn dyeing. Yarn may be dyed before or after it is spun. A technique called space dyeing permits the application of two or more colors to yarn that has been chemically treated to receive different dyes in different areas.

Piece dyeing. This method of dyeing is used after a rug or carpet is completed to achieve a solid color. In cross-dyeing the yarns in a rug or carpet are treated before weaving with different chemicals that are only compatible with certain dyes. After weaving, the rug or carpet is then dipped in from one to five dye baths to obtain patterns with up to five colors.

Printing. Colors are printed only after a rug or carpet has been completed.

Durability and Texture

In addition to the construction and fiber used, one of the most important criteria in judging the durability of a carpet or rug is its density. This is derived from the ply (number of strands used to make a single yarn), from the size and weight (or denier) of the yarn, and from the thickness of the pile (the number of loops, strands, or tufts per inch). The thicker the pile, the less weight each strand of yarn must bear. Carpeting should be tightly packed, and the backing should not be visible through the pile. Bend back a corner of the carpet; the visible backing (or the "grin," as it is called) should be minimal.

Both the appearance and wearability of carpets or rugs are also affected by physical aspects of their texture. The most common textures are described in the chart on the previous page.

What About Fibers?

In either carpets or rugs, the choice of fiber used has a direct bearing on appearance, price, resiliency, and ease of maintenance. Study the chart on the facing page that compares the features of wool, nylon, polyester, polypropylene, and acrylic. Remember that there is a range of quality and price within each fiber category, and be sure to check the samples by bending the carpet back to examine the amount of "grin," as described earlier.

Padding

Padding should always be used under a rug or carpet, unless a carpet is already foam backed. Good padding can lengthen the life of a rug or carpet by at least 50 percent, while adding extra buoyance and comfort at the same time. Padding also provides more thermal insulation, increases the acoustical properties of the rug or carpet, and prevents it from shifting on the floor, which can be a real safety hazard. When selecting a pad, be sure it is soft and firm enough to prevent stretching of the rug or carpet when weight is applied. It should also be resilient enough to spring back to shape when any weight is removed.

The most buoyantly luxurious padding is made of foam rubber or urethane foam. Urethane costs less than rubber and has better resistance to moisture and general deterioration. Flatter hair or fiber felt, or hair-and-fiber pads will also protect a rug or carpet, but they will not add buoyancy. Solid fiber felt is the least durable of all padding.

Traditional Rugs

In traditional decorating Oriental rugs have the longest history, which began with the first small and precious examples brought back from the Orient by early traders. Until the mid-eighteenth

Fiber Chart

Fiber	Trade Names	Resiliency or Crush Resistance	Soil Resistance	Abrasion Resistance	Cost Range	Characteristics
WOOL	**Not applicable**	**Excellent**	**Excellent, but harder to clean than synthetics**	**Excellent**	**High**	**Warm, soft, luxurious appearance and feel. Broad selection of colors and textures.**
NYLON	**Antron Anso Enkalon Ultron Zeftron**	**Excellent**	**Excellent, if static resistant substances added in manufacturing process.**	**Excellent**	**Moderate to high**	**Soft, looks like wool. Wide range of colors, and excellent color retention. Easy to clean.**
POLYESTER	**Dacron Fortrel Trevira**	**Good**	**Good, but particularly susceptible to oily stains.**	**Good**	**Moderate**	**Soft and looks like wool, but cooler to the touch than other fibers; good color retention; little pilling; sheds moisture.**
POLY-PROPYLENE (or Olefin)	**Herculon Marvess Marquesa-Lana Vectra**	**Poor to good**	**Excellent, resists most stains**	**Excellent**	**Low to moderate**	**Limited color choice but improving. Low, uni-level loop constructions are best for broadloom because this fiber has less crush resistance than others, especially if the pile is light. Hard-wearing, both indoors and out, with the appropriate backing.**
ACRYLIC	**Acrilan Badische Acrylic**	**Good**	**Fair to good**	**Fair to good**	**High**	**No longer used for broadloom carpets, but still good for area rugs. Looks like wool and made in many colors. May pill, easy to clean.**

Types of Traditional Rugs	Care Tips
ORIENTAL Genuine Oriental rugs are hand-knotted in the Middle East, India, China, and Russia, and are costly. Oriental-*design* rugs are decorative, less expensive, and not a value investment. Genuine Orientals are usually made of wool; Oriental-design rugs may be made of wool and acrylic, nylon, olefin, or cotton.	Use thin carpet padding, about one inch smaller all around than the rug. Clean professionally. Home cleaning may cause the colors to bleed.
BRAIDED Once handcrafted, these rugs are usually machine-made today. The braiding may be tubular with a thick, cushiony core at the center of each strip in the braid, or flat, which is usually longer wearing. Often identified by ply (the number of strips in the braid)—the higher the ply, the more durable the rug. Check for strong stitching connecting the braids. Available in blends of wool, nylon, acrylic, cotton, and rayon.	Many are washable. Use thick detergent lather; rinse with a damp cloth; blot; vacuum when dry. Alternatively, have the rug cleaned professionally.
HOOKED These rugs are made by hooking yarn into a canvas backing to form a scenic, floral, or geometric pattern. The pile may be looped for a flat look or cut for a plush effect. Rug-hooking kits with prestamped designs can be purchased by the do-it-yourselfer. Available in wool, wool blends, acrylic, and mod-acrylic.	Clean professionally. Home cleaning may cause the pattern to bleed into the background.
RAG Today there is renewed interest in rag rugs, which were originally handmade from cloth strips during Colonial times. Most are still handwoven, usually of multicolor cotton-fabric strips, which produces a ridged texture with a varied, colorful effect. Reversible.	Clean professionally.

century, Oriental rugs were used to cover tables rather than floors because they were so highly prized. Antique handwoven and dyed Orientals have certainly skyrocketed in price at present, but some machine-made versions that have the same traditional designs and nearly the same mellow colors are acceptable substitutes if you can't afford the real things. The chart tells you what to look for in newly made Oriental and other traditional types of rugs.

With any degree of skill, you can also make your own— braided, hooked, and rag rugs, as well as those of a more formal and sophisticated nature in needlepoint and gros point.

Stenciled floors and floor cloths, popular during early Colonial times and now being revived, offer another opportunity for self-expression. See the section on stenciling in Chapter 4, which explains the method of adding pattern to floors or fabrics and tells how to make a floor cloth of any size.

OPPOSITE PAGE:

In traditional decorating, Oriental rugs have long been favored for their rich patterns and colors. They are particularly handsome on old wood floors because the rich character of the wood around them emphasizes their strong decorative element. If an antique handmade Oriental is beyond your budget, you can find some machine-made versions that approximate the same traditional designs and mellow colors.

CHAPTER SEVEN

Walls and ceilings

Everything described so far regarding color, pattern, and texture and their visual effects can be directly applied to your choice of wall and ceiling treatments. Taking these aspects into consideration, the material you select will express the look you want to achieve, in addition to the degree of permanence you expect and the amount of maintenance you are willing to give.

Types of Wall Treatments

There are three basic types of wall treatments: wood paneling, wallpaper, and paint. If the rich look of wood-grained paneling is your choice, you can take your pick of factory-made and prefinished 4-foot-by-8-foot sheets of solid hardwood, veneered or printed plywood, or printed hardboard. Most are plastic-coated for easy maintenance and are far less expensive to install than plank paneling, which must be applied board by board. Either factory-made or natural plank paneling is available in a variety of wood grains that will add a natural warmth to walls. Plank paneling must be sealed with a clear varnish or other sealant or, if preferred, it can first be stained to deepen its natural color or a new color can be added without destroying the grain pattern. Once it is installed and protected by varnish or stain, wood paneling will last for generations.

A greater variety of pattern, color, and texture is available in wallpaper than in any other medium, and it contributes enormously to the overall ambiance of any room. Less expensive to

OPPOSITE PAGE:

During the early part of the nineteenth century, itinerant mural painters journeyed from house to house painting scenes to the owner's order. This contemporary mural of a New England harbor is faithful to the traditional style of mural painting.

install than paneling, wallpaper usually lasts for several years. Except for the most delicate types, most can be carefully wiped clean, and the heavier vinyls are completely scrubbable.

Unlike paneling or wallpaper, paint is the quickest and least expensive way to add fresh color to your walls and ceilings, and when you use paint, you can afford to change your mind every few years without damaging your budget.

Fabric is another alternative to covering a wall that adds warmth and a modicum of sound-proofing at the same time. Expensive or difficult-to-handle fabrics should be installed by a professional, but sheeting and less expensive fabrics can be successfully glued in place with liquid starch or they can be stapled. This treatment is especially suitable for bedrooms.

Wallpaper in American History

Prior to the introduction of wallpaper, colonial walls were paneled, painted, hung with fabric, decorated with stenciling, or simply whitewashed. The advertisement of a Boston merchant in 1700 for "painted paper," from the French *papier peint,* is the earliest record of wallpaper offered for sale in the colonies. Before 1760 most wallpaper came from England, some from the Orient, and some from France. English paper was considered so superior that it was even imported by the French court until the late eighteenth century, when French papers equalled or sometimes surpassed it in quality.

Our independence from England ended British trading restrictions to the colonies, and in 1787 the French removed export duties to our country. Perhaps in gratitude for their help during our revolution, America's wallpaper trade turned to France. While in Paris in 1790, Thomas Jefferson ordered, for Monticello, plain blue and plain scarlet papers along with drapery patterns printed on matching backgrounds, as well as brick and valance patterns.

The influence of Chinese design was very strong from the late seventeenth through the nineteenth centuries. The Chinese produced hand-painted scenic murals and florals, usually made in sets of twenty or twenty-five nonrepeating panels. Sometimes mounted on silk and rolled like a scroll painting for shipping, each set was unique and, because the sets were not made in multiples, they were quite expensive.

The earliest English wallpapers were block-printed in one color, using printer's ink on raised designs carved into a wooden block. By the mid-eighteenth century, a water-based medium of glue or sizing was used to carry pigments, and block printing became multicolored, with a separate block for each color in the design. More expensive varnish-based colors were used for flocked papers; the background was first applied, and then a highly adhesive varnish was used to block-print the pattern before feeding the paper through a trough filled with powdered wood shavings. By 1756 paper was being stamped and printed

OPPOSITE PAGE:

One of the most effective ways to dramatize a ceiling is by adding skylights. They provide an ever-changing view of treetops and stars and, of course, warm sunlight for thriving plants. They can also be covered, if desired, with tailored shades to control the light. Fine old quilts, coverlet upholstery on the armchair, and a rug on the painted floor all add traditional pattern to this otherwise all-white bedroom.

by colonists in the English manner. Using imported patterns as models, the so-called "paper stainers" flourished in New York and other larger settlements.

Popular designs of the eighteenth century included flocked, chinoiserie, florals, sprig, and geometric, as well as architectural motifs, such as arches, columns, decorative plaster motifs, paneling, borders, florals, and plain colors. Plain paper, used with decorative paper swags, moldings, or trelliswork—even statues—was popular from the late eighteenth into the nineteenth century. The most popular colors were sky blue and pea green, followed by yellow, black-and-white, French gray, pink, salmon, and straw. Panoramic papers were popular during the early part of the nineteenth century, with such classic scenes as Roman ruins, monuments of Paris, and the bay of Naples. But only the wealthy could afford such extravagant wall coverings; the middle class hired itinerant mural painters who hand-painted scenes to order for much less than the cost of wallpaper.

It was also during this period that many patterns were printed for use on bandboxes, named for their original use of storing gentlemen's collar bands. These lightweight wood or cardboard boxes were made in oval or round shapes in many different sizes and were used for closet storage or as a catchall for traveling, much as we carry totes or shopping bags today. By the late nineteenth century many paper printers devoted themselves exclusively to bandbox production; their patterns included florals, scenics, commemoratives, even advertisements for their own establishments, just as large stores now promote themselves on their shopping bags.

The first machinery for making endless rolls of paper was patented in England in 1799, and the first American wallpaper mill was established in Delaware in 1817. During the first quarter of the nineteenth century, incised cylinders replaced the blocks used for handprinting, and by 1840 machine production was well under way. The same method of roller printing is still being used but with improved high-speed presses, inks, papers, and protective finishes that range from gently washable to completely scrubbable vinyl wall coverings. Handprinted patterns are still available and can even be colored to your specification, but the cost is considerably higher than the machine-made variety.

During the past few decades the wall-covering industry has made it far easier for do-it-yourselfers. Machine-made papers are usually pretrimmed, eliminating the need to remove the selvage, and many come prepasted, in rolls or squares, to dip in water and apply to a wall. And if you expect to move, heavy grades of strippable paper are available that can be peeled from walls to be reapplied in your new home.

Among these machine-made papers you will find a variety of traditional early American patterns, plus countless simulations of timeless textures, such as burlap, suede, grasscloth, ticking, and even brick, fieldstone, and marble.

OPPOSITE PAGE:

Paint is the easiest, least expensive way to gain a fresh look in a room. In the foyer of this older house, bold green moldings add pattern, and a sky-blue ceiling dotted with trompe l'oeil clouds create the illusion of looking through a skylight.

Traditional Wallcovering Patterns

Formal floral

English floral

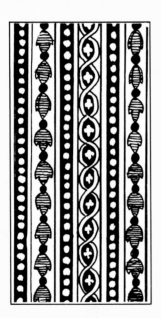

Cable design

Early block print

Borders

India-inspired print

Chinese-inspired print

Geometric design

Sprig pattern

Flocked print

Allover pattern

Fabric-Covered Walls

Wallpaper dealers also offer natural materials such as burlap, silk, felt, grasscloth, and sliver-thin cork bonded to paper for easy installation. Most of these materials come in a rainbow of colors and add a warm look to a wall.

For a completely coordinated bedroom, the walls and ceiling can be covered with the same sheet pattern used on the bed. Yard for yard, sheets are a great buy in both pattern and color, and they are not too difficult to apply. Of course, any other sturdy, closely woven fabric of similar weight will do just as well.

Sheets can be stapled directly to walls made of sheetrock, wood, or plaster, or they can be glued to smooth walls of any type with liquid starch. Stapling is the quickest way, particularly if you want to achieve a shirred effect that more or less eliminates the careful matching of pattern. The stapling method also tends to conceal any imperfections in the wall surface, whereas gluing will strictly conform to every bump.

Whichever method you use, cut sheet panels to the height of the wall, allowing a 1½-inch excess at the top and bottom for easier handling. Be sure to match the pattern as each panel is aligned. If the selvage edge has been distorted in printing, remove it or turn it under. Use pushpins across the top to hold each panel in place as you work.

To staple fabric, start at a corner and apply staples at two- or three-inch intervals across the top of a panel, leaving the excess fabric to be trimmed off later. Then pull the fabric smooth and taut and staple it across the bottom; staple along one side and then the other, pulling the fabric smooth as you go along. If you want the pattern to match exactly, each panel can overlap the preceding panel, or the edge can be folded under the necessary amount. Use a metal ruler to guide you in cutting off the excess at the top and bottom with a razor-edged knife. If the staples are conspicuous, a tape or braid in a coordinating color can be tacked or glued over them.

If the fabric is to be glued to the wall with liquid starch, first scrub the walls thoroughly to remove any traces of dirt and grease. Then cover the floor with a sheet of plastic to protect it from spills. Using a sponge, apply starch to the top of one wall at a corner. Press the top of a fabric panel in place, leaving an excess of 1½ inches across the top, and secure the panel with push pins. Work your way down the panel a few feet at a time, applying a generous coating of starch and smoothing the fabric into place. Then, using a brushing motion, smooth a coating of starch on top of the finished panel to remove any wrinkles or bubbles; this surface coating creates a smoother application and adds a soil-resistant finish to the fabric. After the starch is thoroughly dry, cut off the excess fabric at top and bottom. If some bubbles have appeared, soak them with starch and smooth them out. If you want to remove the sheeting or other fabric at a later date, simply moisten it with a damp sponge, and peel it off.

OPPOSITE PAGE:

Sheets provide an inexpensive means of coordinating a bedroom. In this example they are used to slipcover a chair, cover a window seat, and line an armoire, in addition to covering the bed, walls, and ceilings. The remaining decorating decisions are relatively easy to make because everything else ties into the basic theme.

Paint

Our ancestors made their own paint by coloring a buttermilk base with natural dyes, or they used whitewash made from a mixture of slaked lime and water. Today you can still buy a buttermilk-based paint in authentic colonial colors, but if they had been given the opportunity, chances are that our ancestors would have opted for today's improved paints now available in every conceivable color or even mixed to specific order. The authentic colors used in Williamsburg, Charleston, and other

The ultimate in transforming blank wall space is probably trompe l'oeil painting. Here it is used to turn a plain kitchen cabinet into a window on a garden. Except for the simple free-hand painting of the flowers and false hardware, the rest of the execution can be simply accomplished with the help of masking tape to create straight lines.

Soft wall colors dramatize the furniture, flattering the warm wood tones and silhouetting the upholstered pieces.

Furniture becomes less important visually with darker walls that neither contrast nor relate to the wood or fabric tones.

If you want to draw attention to such architectural features as paneling or molding, paint them a contrasting color.

historic areas are also available, if you choose to be absolutely accurate in creating a period room.

Except for special purposes, oil-based paints have largely been replaced by latex and alkyd enamel. You can choose a flat, semi-gloss, or high-gloss finish in either type. Water-based latex paint is easy to apply and it dries almost immediately. It is also easy to clean the paint from brushes and rollers and to clean up spills with water. In addition, the paint is practically odorless, and it can be used on almost any surface.

Alkyd enamel has a synthetic resin base, is nearly odorless and takes a bit longer to dry, but it creates a tougher surface. Because of its superior cleanability and moisture resistance, alkyd high-gloss enamel is the best choice for soil-prone surfaces that require frequent scrubbing, as do most woodwork and walls in children's rooms, kitchens, and baths. It is also glossier than a glossy latex paint.

Whichever paint you choose, the finest finish you can give it is with a brush; rollers always leave a stipple effect. However, it is quickest to apply the paint with a roller and then brush over it.

Which finish to use. A flat-finish paint will absorb the most light, intensifying the color. Glossy paint is the most highly reflective and thus the brightest, and semi-gloss offers a compromise between the light-absorbing and highly reflective extremes. In terms of scrubbability, high-gloss rates the best followed by semi-gloss and flat matte in descending order. In most rooms the walls are normally painted with a matte finish and the woodwork with a semigloss. High-gloss is reserved for baths, kitchens, and children's rooms, as already mentioned.

Tricks with Paint

Darker, more vibrant colors advance toward the eye; because they are more demanding, they seem to shrink the dimensions of a room.

Ceiling too low? White, or a pale tint of a wall color, lifts the eye upward, making the ceiling seem much higher than it really is.

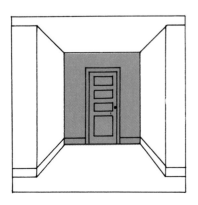

Pale, tranquil colors are inobtrusive, leading the eye into the distance and increasing the apparent size of the room.

If the ceiling is too high, its apparent height can be lowered by painting it several shades darker than the color used on the walls.

The dimensions of a long and too narrow room or hallway can appear wider if a stronger color is used on the shorter end walls.

Tricks with paint. The paint colors you choose can fool the eye and change the architectural appearance of a room. Ceiling too low? White or a pale tint of the wall color will lift it. A too-high ceiling can be lowered by painting it several shades darker than the wall color, or can be made to recede by painting it the exact color of your walls.

If a long and narrow room is your problem, solve it by using a stronger color on the two shorter walls to seemingly bring them closer together. If you are lucky enough to have a handsome mantlepiece or fine moldings around windows and doorways, dramatize these attractive architectural features by painting them a color that contrasts with the walls. Conversely, unattractive architectural features will seem to vanish if painted the color of walls.

The small paint-chip samples available from a dealer can give you an idea of which colors you want but not a clear picture of how a color will actually look on a wall. Before investing in enough paint for an entire room, buy just one can and cover a large area on two adjoining walls; this will bounce enough light on the color at different times of the day to give you a good idea of the final result.

Special effects with paint. To create a stuccolike provincial texture, brush on a latex-based paint that includes silica sand. For a two-color effect with both pattern and texture, apply a base coat of the stronger color; when the base is completely dry, apply a thicker coat of the second color and, while it is still wet, dab on a pattern of small dots with a stippling brush, or dab with a sponge for a larger mottled effect. You can also run a heavy comb across the wet surface in any pattern that pleases you—swirls, cross-hatches, horizontal or vertical lines, blocks, or diamond shapes. A paint dealer can supply the necessary materials for these special effects, and it's highly advisable to experiment on a wide board before tackling a wall to make sure you really like the effect.

Contemporary architecture can be given a traditional treatment with period furniture and wall treatment. The vertically striped wallpaper below the chair rail is reminiscent of wainscoting, and the darker companion paper above it unifies the room and also helps to make the space seem cozier. Only the lower portion of the floor-to-ceiling window is curtained for privacy; the clerestory window is left bare.

CHAPTER EIGHT

Selecting new furniture

More than anything else, furniture establishes the style of a room. In addition, it may represent the biggest decorating expenditure. When you buy a sofa or a dining-room table and chairs, it is fairly certain that you will be living with them for some time. For this reason it's important to choose carefully, but you shouldn't worry about your choice if you know what to look for.

There are five important factors to be considered in the selection of new furniture: style, scale, suitability, comfort, and construction. Style is visible at a glance and can be roughly divided into traditional and contemporary. Exact reproductions of popular traditional furniture are almost certain to be of good design, if only because the style has survived the taste test of so many generations. Adaptations of period styles, often scaled down for modern rooms, can also be pleasingly suitable.

If you love a period style just the way it is, and if it fits in with your family's way of life, by all means adopt it. You can decorate entirely with antiques, if you can afford them, with reproductions or adaptations, or with a mixture of the old and the new. It's also fun to mix styles, either because they're so similar that they live well together or for the exact opposite reason—because the contrast provides excitement. The one rule is to choose pieces that have the same basic feeling—formal or informal, striking or serene.

Scale, of course, refers to a proper relation in terms of size—a small room will look larger if small-scale furniture is used in it.

OPPOSITE PAGE:

An eclectic mix of antique country furniture approximates the look of an early American great room where the family lived and dined near the warmth of an open hearth. The top of the hutch table lifts, when not in use for dining, to become a high-backed chair.

Wicker furniture could be found in every Victorian era home from the nursery to the porch, and it is still prized in very different settings, both traditional and modern.

Folk art decoration is a part of the rich design heritage brought by emigrants from Europe. On this beautifully detailed chest, done in the Pennsylvania Dutch tradition, bands of stylized flowers separate painted panels decorated with distelfinks, the Pennsylvania Dutch term for birds.

Suitability refers to your way of life—formal or informal—as well as to the degree of maintenance you can provide. Working mothers, for example, will want to keep chores to a minimum and may prefer to choose "childproof" furnishings. Construction is difficult to assess at a glance, but the life of your furniture hinges on good construction. Since your investment in furniture could be considerable, it is wise to look for quality in both upholstered and all-wood pieces.

Quality in Wood Furniture

All wood furniture is now called "case goods" by the industry, although traditionally chairs were not considered case goods. Wood furniture is the easiest to judge in terms of both style and construction. Chairs, tables, desks, cabinets of all types, settles—anything that is not upholstered—declares its style by its design and the type of hardware used, if any. Unlike covered upholstered furniture, you can closely examine case goods to determine how and of what material they are made.

The cost of wood furniture is determined by the kind of wood used, the quality of construction, the type of finish, the number of manufacturing processes involved, the amount of hand labor required to produce the item, and the amount of material wasted in the process of manufacture. As a result of these considerations there may be a tremendous difference between a fine piece of furniture and a quality piece. Each may be well constructed and of good quality, but the laborious finishing process, the kind of wood used, or the construction details could alter the price considerably.

Basic furniture materials include hardwoods from deciduous leaf-bearing trees such as maple, walnut, oak, pecan, mahogany, cherry, and birch and less expensive softwoods from pine, cedar, fir, and other evergreen needle-bearing trees. Wood substitutes include particle board, made of fine flakes of wood with a resin binding, and hardboard made of pressed wood fibers. Particle board surfaces are covered with thin sheets of veneer sliced from natural hardwood. Hardboard, on the other hand, can be printed with a natural grain and then finished to look like natural wood.

Solid Versus Veneer Wood

The early cabinetmakers made their furniture of solid wood and sometimes used a contrasting hardwood veneer for inlaid decoration. With the advent of machine-made furniture in the nineteenth century, hardwood veneer was often used to cover furniture made of less expensive softwood, particularly during our late Federal period when mirror frames, head and foot boards for beds, tables, and other pieces were often veneered ineptly, causing the veneer to warp or crack and eventually

Spool-turned furniture, extremely popular during the ninteenth century, represented a resurgence of the seventeenth-century style of bulbous-turned furniture. Although generally called "spool," the category also includes the more common bulb, ball, and button shapes, which were used in this antique crib and four-poster bed.

Hoop-back Windsor chairs contrast gracefully with the rectangular lines of the harvest furniture table and primitive dresser in this authentically styled dining room. A collection of hearth brooms hangs from Shaker pegs.

drop off completely. Today's superior adhesives and improved manufacturing techniques have virtually eliminated those early problems; modern veneer construction can now add structural strength and beautiful graining for less than the cost of solid wood.

Today the strength of a veneered piece is gained by permanently bonding a five-layer "sandwich" consisting of a thick particle-board core in the center, thinner cross bands of wood at either side of the core, and face and back veneer at the top and bottom. The cross banding of wood grains on the thinner strips provides stability and limits expansion and contraction of the particle-board core. Thus veneer construction costs less than solid wood, is stronger, and the face veneer can equal in every way the appearance of more expensive solid wood.

The term *solid-wood construction* can only be used when all the exposed parts of a piece of furniture are made of solid wood

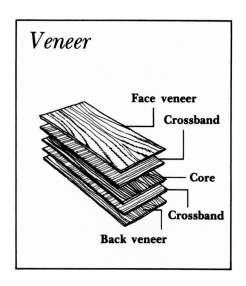

Veneer

Face veneer
Crossband
Core
Crossband
Back veneer

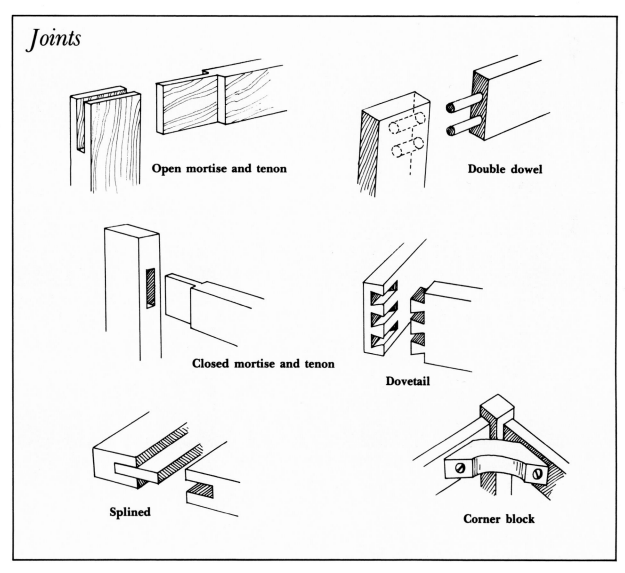

Joints

Open mortise and tenon

Double dowel

Closed mortise and tenon

Dovetail

Splined

Corner block

Questions to Ask When Buying New Furniture:

■ **Will the furniture be used by children, adults, or both?**

■ **Will pets be on the furniture?**

■ **How much do you want to spend?**

■ **Do you want a piece of furniture to last a long time or only a few years?**

■ **Will the furniture be easy to move?**

■ **How many functions should the piece of furniture satisfy?**

It is always exciting to find a new and imaginative use for a piece of furniture that others might consider worthless. The big cabinet in this collector's kitchen was originally made for use in a hotel dining room; its drawers and cupboards now store cookware and dinnerware; collectibles are displayed on the shelves.

without a veneer facing; interior parts, however, may be made of particle board, plywood, hardboard, or other material. Most pieces of furniture carry hang tags or labels to identify the woods and/or veneers used in their construction.

Each piece of furniture is made in separate parts—arms, legs, stretchers, backs, fronts, sides, tops, drawer parts—that fit together with special joints such as dovetail, mortise-and-tenon, dowel, or tongue-and-groove, depending on the nature of the piece, and the joints may be reinforced with glue, screws, or nails, alone or in combination, and perhaps a reinforcing wood block.

The best quality furniture is made of the finest solid wood and the most beautiful veneers finished with meticulous care to bring out the beauty of the natural grain and wood color and to provide durable construction. Less expensive furniture, which may not hold up as well, is finished to produce pleasing tones that may or may not be natural to the wood but will mask any undesirable grain effects.

Some finishes are "distressed" with dents, wormholes, scratches, and other signs of age to approximate a mellow antique look; distressing of this type tends to disguise signs of normal wear. Some heavy-duty surfaces, such as tabletops and chests, are given plastic-laminate tops that provide the look of wood but are much less vulnerable to stains and scratches. Federal law requires that furniture with plastic components be so identified with a label or tag.

Inspecting Chairs and Tables

Good construction in furniture is determined largely by how well the parts of a piece are joined. Firm and secure joints are required to withstand the strain from weight and movement during use. Look at the underside of a chair or table: The legs should be joined to the top or seat with a corner-block construction. Where screws are used there should be washers to keep the screw away from the wood. Check to be sure there are no spaces or gaps where one piece joins the next.

Test each piece of furniture yourself, using the same amount of stress and strain you expect it to receive during regular use. Place your palms on the opposite sides of a tabletop, and try to rock the table. It should be well balanced so it won't wobble or creak. Sit in a chair and sway back and forth; the chair should be steady and well balanced, with no wobbling or creaking. While sitting in the chair, push at the arms and back; there should be no give.

Feel under the edges of the table apron and the bottom edge of the chair seat; if the surface feels rough, it will snag clothing and hosiery. Check for knee clearance under a table, especially if the table and chairs are not of a matching set. A 7-inch minimum clearance is needed between chair seat and table apron to avoid a tight squeeze.

If you are purchasing an extension table, ask to see the leaves, which are usually not shown with the floor sample. Table leaves should blend in color and graining with the rest of the table. If the table has an apron, the leaves should also have an apron.

Check for chair arm clearance, especially if the chairs and table are not of a matching set. Chair arms should not extend too far out or be so high that it is difficult to pull the chair close to the table. Check for clearance in a desk and chair arrangement too. Finally, if a chair has a saddle or an attached seat, jiggle it firmly to make certain it is securely attached.

Inspecting Large Case Goods

In any piece of furniture, check the fit of all component parts; joints and veneer, if any, should be hairline thin, nearly invisible.

To check a chest of drawers or a cabinet, rap the top and end panels with your knuckles. Thin panels will sound hollow; heavy panels, which add rigidity and durability to a piece, will sound dull. Examine the back; plywood or hardboard back panels are stronger than particle board. On the best furniture, the back panel is also recessed to function as a supporting member.

Make sure that the spacing around a drawer is equal on both sides and across the top, and that the drawer slides out easily and smoothly. Jiggle the drawer from side to side; there should not be more than a quarter-inch of play. Drawers should all line up well and be even, with handles, knobs, or finger grooves evenly placed. Pull out a drawer and look for built-in guiding devices that make for easier sliding. Tightly fitted dovetail joints, with no residual evidence of glue, and waxing inside and out to prevent snagging of delicate clothing are also signs of good drawer construction. Remove all the drawers and look inside the piece to see if dust panels have been provided between each drawer.

If the piece has doors, check to see that they hang squarely and are adequately hinged. The doors should fit snugly when closed and swing open evenly.

Scratch the finish along an edge where molding has been applied: A poor finish will flake off and leave a bare mark. All flat surfaces should feel smooth, with no bumps or grains.

Check the Hardware

Be certain that all hardware is well secured. In well-constructed furniture handles go completely through the wood and are anchored with bolts and washers, not merely nailed on. Hardware should be well finished and have no rough edges. Knobs and handles should fit your hand comfortably. Better quality hardware is cast or stamped out of heavy metal rather

---

Testing a Chair for Comfort

■ **Sit in the chair. If your feet rest flat on the floor and the chair supports your thighs, the chair is well proportioned for you.**

■ **The seat should slant slightly toward the back. A flat seat is often better than the bucket type because it allows more freedom of movement. There should be some clearance from the edge of the chair to the back of your knee.**

■ **The chair should curve in the back or have an opening at the lumbar region to allow room for the buttocks.**

■ **The back of the chair should be slanted to support the lumbar region of your back without causing discomfort to the shoulder blades.**

■ **The arms of the chair should be of proper height to support your arms without causing you to raise your shoulders.**

than simply stamped out of lightweight metal. Some large pieces of furniture should have recessed casters for mobility.

Choosing Upholstered Furniture

As in any decorating purchase, begin by looking for the style that suits you best. Although there are many traditional styles in upholstered pieces—camelback, lawson, chesterfield, and tuxedo sofas and wing-back chairs—comfort should be your most important consideration; your choice of upholstery fabric can add a traditional look to a comfortable contemporary piece.

Size is also important. A sofa and two upholstered chairs are considered the nucleus of an average-size living-room arrangement. If the room is small, a loveseat would be a better choice than a sofa; in a large room you might want to use a sofa, a loveseat, and two chairs, or even large matching sofas. Upholstered chairs should be in scale with the sofa or loveseat, but their fabric need only relate in color and texture rather than match exactly.

Unless you buy a floor sample for immediate delivery, a wide choice of upholstery fabric is available. And, because the manufacturer will upholster the piece with the fabric of your choice, whether you choose it in the store or provide it from another source, delivery may take from one to three months.

Judging Upholstered Furniture

The quality of upholstered furniture is defined largely by its construction, and there are five basic features to consider when making a selection: the frame, springs, webbing, cushioning material, and fiberfill. Because you can't see it, construction is difficult to check. Tags and labels will identify the wood used for the frame as well as materials used in cushioning and filling. Forearmed with a little knowledge, you can ask the salesman to tell you which type of construction was used.

Frame. In better pieces the frame is made of seasoned hardwood, preferably birch, soft maple, sycamore, or gum, with corner blocks, screwed in place, added to reinforce double-doweled joints.

Springs. Coiled spring construction of the platform (or seat) contributes to the degree of comfort. Eight-way hand-tied coil springs of tempered wire are the best and the most luxuriously comfortable. They should be close to each other, but not touching, and should be sewn to the webbing or stapled to the sides. Wire-linked coil springs are the next best; and arched sinuous springs are reasonably comfortable and the least expensive. Coil springs should be oven-japanned, which looks like black paint on high-carbon steel.

The best-made backs may have pocketed coil construction in

Upholstery Construction

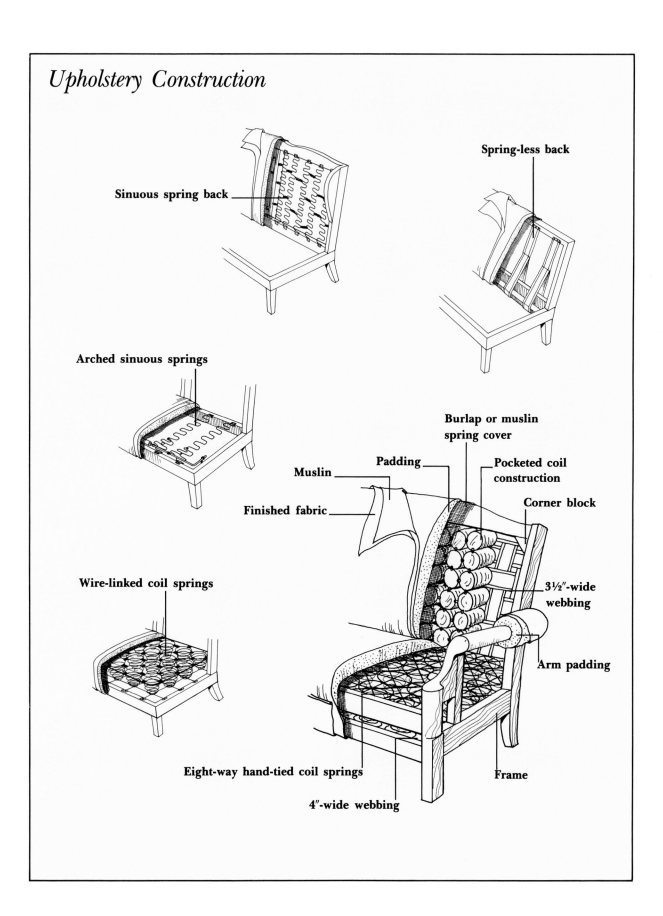

Sinuous spring back

Spring-less back

Arched sinuous springs

Burlap or muslin
spring cover

Padding

Muslin

Pocketed coil
construction

Finished fabric

Corner block

3½″-wide
webbing

Wire-linked coil springs

Arm padding

Eight-way hand-tied coil springs

Frame

4″-wide webbing

If you delight in the heritage of stately living that dates back to the eighteenth century, this room approximates that gracious style of formal living. The newly made furniture is based on the still popular Queen Anne style but is slightly smaller for modern use. Pull-out shelves on the tea table serve their original purpose of holding candles.

which each coil is sewn into an individual fabric pocket. A sinuous spring back, with vertical springs arched into the frame and cross-linked with tightly coiled springs or wires, is comfortable and less expensive. A back without springs of any kind is used when loose cushions provide comfort. In this kind of construction either webbing or a tough fabric is pulled taut over the hollow back frame, and cotton padding is added before the piece is upholstered.

Webbing. Sometimes you can see the webbing beneath the seat; in better construction it will be made of closely interlaced and tightly stretched 4-inch-wide strips of jute marked with red lines. On less expensive pieces, it will be more widely spaced. The webbing used on backs is marked with black lines and is 3½ inches wide. Construction that uses nonsag units or support slats of any kind is inferior.

Cushioning materials and fiberfill. These refer to the materials applied directly over the springs and frame and the protective padding between the cushioning materials and the outer fabric. How they are used, individually and in combination, determines quality. In the best quality seat-cushion construction, individual coil springs are encased in fabric pockets and then covered with urethane foam and an additional layer of down and feathers or polyester fiber. A seat cushion constructed of a layer of firm urethane and two layers of softer foam covered with a final wrapping of polyester fiber is less expensive. In the most common and least expensive construction of all, a core of dense urethane foam with a polyester-fiberfill wrap provides firm support as well as surface softness.

Back pillows are usually filled with polyester fiber or ground polyurethane foam contained within a ticking under the upholstery fabric. Natural down pillows, still available on special order, provide the deepest comfort, but they cost a lot and you will have to plump them back into shape between sittings. A combination of down and polyester fiber also costs more, but it is almost equally comfortable and keeps its shape more successfully than pure down.

Try before you buy. You will, of course, be attracted by style and fabric, but don't buy an upholstered piece before testing it for comfort. First, an upholstered item must be well padded, with no lumps or bumps; you should not be able to feel the framework through the upholstery. Push at the arms and back of the chair or sofa. If the frame gives, it is defective. If possible, lift up the sofa or chair by one end to determine if the frame is secure. There should be no movement or shifting.

Then sit full in the chair or sofa with your back touching the back. If the fit is good you should be able to touch your heels on the floor without straining, and you should feel full and even support along your thighs. Still sitting, keep your arms against your body but extend your hand and forearm. Ideally, the chair

An early pine corner cupboard, an old wooden filing cabinet, and two tables in similar finishes provide the strongest warm tones in this neutral color scheme. The wing chair, one of the most popular pieces in many traditional rooms, forms a bold counterpoint to the cleverly stenciled, rug-shaped pattern on the floor.

arms should be about one inch higher than your elbow—this height allows leverage for shifting your body weight and good shoulder support when you lean.

Most people sit first on the front edge of a chair and then lower themselves fully into the seat. Run your hands over the chair seat and press down heavily. The front edge should be firmer to take your body weight when you sit on it (and also to support your weight when you get up). The rear (about four to seven inches from the back) should be softer and have more give, because this area bears most of the body weight.

Now check the tailoring. Look for straight seams and straight welt cording. There should be no loose threads, and patterns on separate panels should match up well. The skirt should be sewn on straight, and it should hang evenly and have an inner lining to hold it straight and prevent wrinkling. In medium and low-priced furniture, skirts are often machine-stapled to the piece. Buttons should be hand-sewn through the filling, not merely tacked on.

Upholstery Fabrics

In selecting fabrics, just as in selecting furniture, begin by looking for the style that you feel works best with your traditional decorating choices. For a formal look, choose tightly woven damasks, velvets, silks; plaids, checks, and sprigged and larger florals are usually less formal. For really heavy-duty upholstery, vinyls come in marvelous colors and patterns, including look-alike leather. Better quality vinyls are fabric-backed for tear resistance, and you can expect them to wear like iron.

Fabric grades. Stores offer upholstery-fabric choices in books of swatches arranged in alphabetical or numerical grades starting with A or 1, the least expensive, and continuing with as many grades or price levels as the manufacturer offers. Higher grades may not be as serviceable as lower ones, and because an average-size sofa requires between 12 and 14 yards of fabric, the choice of a higher grade can add considerably to the cost of the piece. There are a number of factors that affect the quality—and generally the resulting price—of a fabric.

Wearability. The durability of a fabric depends on both fiber content (listed on the tag or label) and the type of weave used—the tighter it is, the tougher the wear. Tightly woven cottons and synthetics, or a blend of both, are available in the lower price ranges and they will wear longer than more loosely woven textures that may separate somewhat with wear. The following chart of fibers and their characteristics will help when you shop for upholstered furniture.

Check the way in which a fabric responds to use. Pull at a fabric swatch in all directions to be certain the fabric holds its

In a collector's treasure-filled dining room, excellent reproductions of Shaker chairs, with typical seats made of woven tape, surround a table top newly made of two wide mahogany boards. The antique apothecary chest with labeled drawers is filled with old drug jars. Simple window draperies repeat the pattern of the wall covering.

OPPOSITE PAGE:

You need not be limited to antiques in your search for period furniture; good reproductions or adaptations for modern use can be found to suit almost any "period" look you might want. In this formal living room the exposed-frame sofa is French in feeling, the sideboard is Georgian in style, and the coffee-table—a modern concept in terms of size—is an adaptation of English styles.

Fibers Used in Upholstery and Slipcovers

Fiber	Some Trade Names	Characteristics
NYLON	**Anso** **Antron** **Enka** **Enkalon** **Ultron** **Zeftron**	**Excellent for rugged wear (family rooms) because it's the most abrasive-resistant fiber.** **Often blended with other fibers to add strength.** **Dyes to many colors and can be made in a variety of textures.**
OLEFIN OR POLYPROPYLENE	**Herculon** **Vectra**	**Exceptionally stain resistant; almost any stain washes off if attended to promptly, and so fabrics require no special stain-resistant finish.** **Excellent abrasion resistance (second only to nylon).**
COTTON		**Dyes and prints beautifully, can be made up in all kinds of fabrics, lightweight to heavy.** **Has a natural look and a soft, comfortable feel.** **Abrasion resistance depends on fabric type—good if heavy and tightly woven.**
RAYON	**Avril** **Fibro**	**Inexpensive. Solution-dyed has best colorfastness.** **Low abrasion resistance.** **Used mostly in blends for color and/or texture.**
ACETATE	**Chromspun** **Coloray**	**Comparatively inexpensive but tends to fade unless solution-dyed.** **Low abrasion resistance.** **Used in blends, adds sheen to satins, damasks, velvets.**
ACRYLIC	**Acrilan** **Creslan** **Orlon**	**Good resiliency and resists matting. Often used for pile fabrics—fake furs, plushes, velvets.** **Can also be made to resemble wool tweed.** **Good abrasion resistance.**
POLYESTER	**Avlin** **Dacron** **Encron** **Fortrel** **Kodel** **Spectran** **Trevira**	**Good for the new upholstery knits, because it resists sagging and stretching.** **Good abrasion resistance.** **Often blended with cotton to add strength and wrinkle resistance.**
VINYL	**Boltaflex** **Duran** **Naugahyde**	**Very durable, but if punctured can tear, and so it's fabric-backed for tear resistance.** **Highly stain resistant; surface wipes clean easily with sudsy sponge.** **Can resemble leather or fabric; "breathable" vinyls (see label) are the most comfortable.**

shape and does not begin to separate in your fingers. Grip two edges of the swatch and, with thumbs close together, press downward on the fabric as hard as you can and turn the cloth over as you press. A durable fabric will not give way or pull apart under such pressure. Rub the fabric surfaces together. The fabric should not look rubbed and there should be no pills or tiny balls of fabric on the surface. Now hold the fabric swatch up to the light. If the fabric is tightly woven, which is necessary for long wear, you should not see any light between the threads. Any quilting on fabric should be done with locked stitches.

Colorfastness. In very sunny rooms, you can expect some fading. Tests indicate that the brighter the color, the faster it fades. Pure colors (red, yellow, blue) simply get lighter, but mixed colors, such as aqua (blue-green) or purple (red-blue), often change completely when one tone fades more than another. Prints tend to fade more than yarn-dyed designs that are woven in.

Cleanability. Special finishes, such as Scotchgard and Zepel, make fabrics stain resistant, *not* stainproof. These finishes can be applied to all types of fabrics to keep them looking cleaner longer. They will repel oily as well as water-based stains; however, a spill on any fabric should be attended to quickly.

In addition to the preceding features, you should consider the characteristics of the fibers themselves. Study the chart to compare the differences between the most common fibers used in upholstery.

Slipcovers

Slipcovers can give your room an entirely new look, perhaps just for summer alone, as well as lengthen the life of your upholstery fabrics. If you expect to use slipcovers, buy completely upholstered pieces with separate seat and back cushions so that the slipcovers will have a tighter, more tailored fit on individual cushions. Pieces with tufted or channel backs or with an exposed frame are far more difficult to slipcover.

In general, look for medium-weight fabrics, such as chintzes and other cottons and non-wrinkling linens, that are closely woven and will hold up well. Avoid heavy fabrics such as velvet, and stretchy fabrics that are hard to handle and may not wear or clean well. Also bear in mind that slipcovering over velvet may abrade the pile of that fabric. Plain-colored slipcovers often benefit from plain or shirred welting made in a contrasting color, or from substituting an attractive cording or short fringe for the welting. Different effects can also be achieved by the skirt of the slipcover; it may be ruffled, box-pleated, or have kick pleats at the corners. If you wish to leave the frame of the furniture exposed, an upholstered slipcover can be made that fastens neatly under the seat. Velcro fastenings are very satisfactory for this treatment.

Upholstered Chair Skirts

Kick pleat

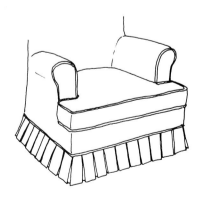

Ruffle

Box pleat

Yardage Chart for Slipcovers Using 48-inch-wide Fabric

Yards of fabric required

Type of Furniture	Number of Cushions	Total Yards of Trimming or Welting Required	Type of Fabric		Fabric for Welting	Type of Skirt		
			Plain	Figured or Striped		Straight	Ruffled	Pleated
SOFA						1½	3	4
	3	46	14	15½	2	—	—	—
	1	33	13½	15	1½	—	—	—
	0	21	10	11	1	—	—	—
LOVE SEAT						1½	2	3
	2	24	10	11	1½	—	—	—
	1	23	10	11	1⅓	—	—	—
	0	14	8½	9¼	1	—	—	—
ARM CHAIR						1	1½	2½
	1	18	7½	8¼	1	—	—	—
	0	13	6	6¾	¾	—	—	—
BOUDOIR CHAIR						1	1½	2½
	1	15	5	5¾	1	—	—	—
	0	12	4½	5¼	¾	—	—	—
WING CHAIR						1	1½	2½
	1	18	8	9	1	—	—	—
	0	13	6½	7¼	¾	—	—	—
DAYBED AND MATTRESS						1½	3	4
	3	42	14½	16	2	—	—	—
	0	27	11	12	1½	—	—	—
DAYBED						1½	3	4
	3	29	11	12	2	—	—	—
	0	14	7½	8¼	1	—	—	—
OTTOMAN	0	6	2	2½	1	1	1½	2½
CHAISE LONGUE						1½	3	4
	1	23	10	11	1½	—	—	—
	0	16	8	9	1	—	—	—
DINING ROOM CHAIR	0	5½	1½	1¾	1	—	—	—
EXTRA CUSHION	1	5	1¼	1¾	1	—	—	—

Yardage Chart for Slipcovers Using 36-inch-wide Fabric

Yards of fabric required

Type of Furniture	Number of Cushions	Total Yards of Trimming or Welting Required	Type of Fabric		Fabric for Welting	Type of Skirt		
			Plain	Figured or Striped		Straight	Ruffled	Pleated
SOFA						2	4½	6
	3	46	21	23	2⅔	—	—	—
	1	33	20½	22½	2	—	—	—
	0	21	15	17	1¼	—	—	—
LOVE SEAT						2	3	4½
	2	24	15	16½	2	—	—	—
	1	23	15	16½	1¾	—	—	—
	0	14	12¾	14¼	1¼	—	—	—
ARM CHAIR						1½	2½	3½
	1	18	11¼	12¼	1¼	—	—	—
	0	13	8½	9½	1	—	—	—
BOUDOIR CHAIR						1½	2½	3½
	1	15	7¾	8¾	1¼	—	—	—
	0	12	6½	7½	1	—	—	—
WING CHAIR						1½	2½	3½
	1	18	12	13½	1¼	—	—	—
	0	13	9¾	10¾	1	—	—	—
DAYBED AND MATTRESS						2	4½	6
	3	42	21¾	23¾	2	—	—	—
	0	27	17½	19½	1¼	—	—	—
DAYBED						2	4½	6
	3	29	16½	18	2⅔	—	—	—
	0	14	11	12¼	1¼	—	—	—
OTTOMAN	0	6	3	3½	1	1½	2½	3½
CHAISE LONGUE						2	3	4½
	1	23	15	16½	2	—	—	—
	0	16	12	13¼	1¼	—	—	—
DINING ROOM CHAIR	0	5½	1⅚	2¼	1	—	—	—
EXTRA CUSHION	1	5	1⅚	2¼	1	—	—	—

CHAPTER NINE

Window treatments

The word for window comes from *vindauga,* a fifteenth-century Norse word combining *vindr* (wind) and *auga* (eye). Back then small openings in walls were intended to ventilate a room and to allow a narrow view of the outside world. If they were covered with anything it was probably animal hide or a heavy fabric to keep out cold and wind.

Windows have probably been around as long as houses; at any rate, we know the ancient Egyptians had them because windows are shown in their wall paintings. The Romans, in the first century, were apparently the first to "glaze" or close these openings with glass. But for centuries thereafter glass was so expensive and so difficult to handle that glazed windows were the exception rather than the rule and were largely confined to the mullioned type—small glass panes held together by lead or wooden strips. Our first glass factory, established in Jamestown, Virginia, in 1610, had a limited production of early window glass of this type.

When improved techniques in glassmaking made it possible to roll the molten material into larger sheets, windows began to expand in size. Today we have a variety of window types and shapes, as well as a number of different decorative choices for treating each type.

OPPOSITE PAGE:

In the dining area of a country kitchen, stenciled tab curtains are used at the small, double-hung window. Since privacy is no problem, the bow window is left uncurtained for an unrestrained view of the garden. The homemade tablecloth, blue-and-white china, and garden-grown marigolds add bright color.

Window Types

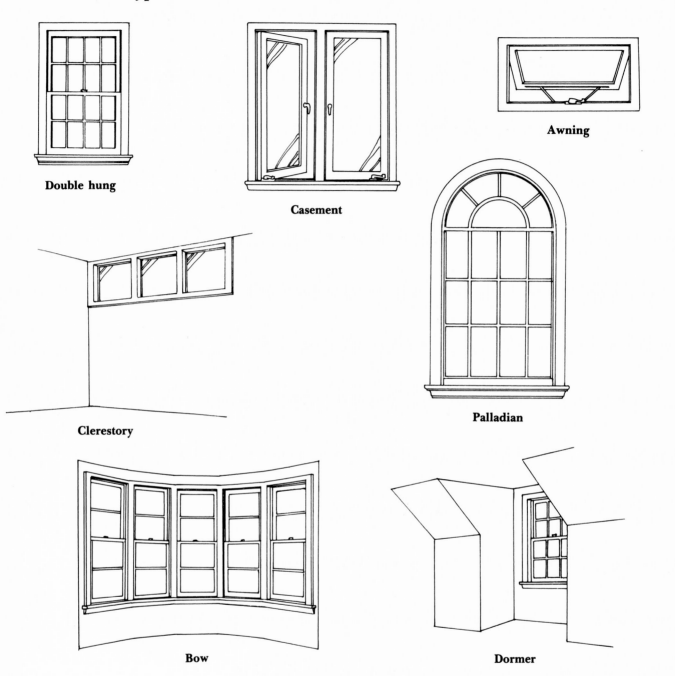

Double hung

Casement

Awning

Clerestory

Palladian

Bow

Dormer

Window Types

A double-hung sash with two large panes of glass, one above and one below, is the most common type of window. Sashes containing smaller panes, like those used in early houses, often with more panes in one sash than the other, are still found in some new colonial-style homes. Windows of this type are referred to as ten-over-twelve, six-over-eight, or however many panes were used for the upper and lower sash.

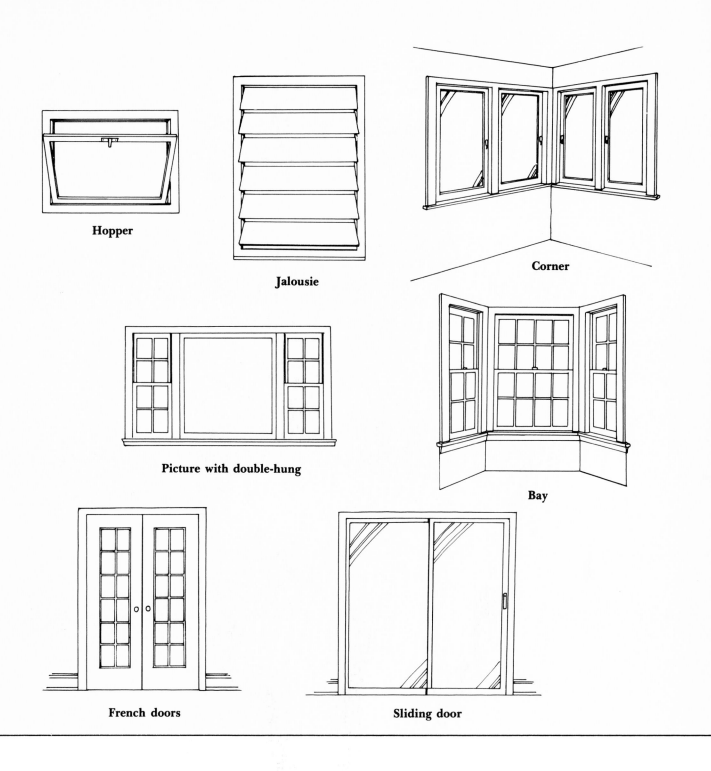

Hopper

Jalousie

Corner

Picture with double-hung

Bay

French doors

Sliding door

Other window types include bay, bow, casement, awning, jalousie, hopper, picture, clerestory, and Palladian (named for the sixteenth-century Italian architect Andrea Palladio who modified classic Roman styles). The biggest windows of all are entire walls of glass that are often punctuated with a sliding glass door that opens onto a terrace or patio. Because they admit light, french doors are also considered to be windows, whether they lead outdoors or open into another room.

Because they admit light, french doors are also considered windows. In this dining room, traverse draperies, topped by a wooden cornice, can be drawn together to cover both doors.

An early Colonial atmosphere is established by wall paneling, wide floor boards, and Queen Anne-style furniture. The simple window treatment—plain floor-length curtains shirred on a rod with embroidered tiebacks—is in keeping with the traditional formality of the room. The long white panels of the curtains also add height and brightness to a relatively small, dark space.

Window Treatments

The basic purpose of a window, of course, is to let in light and air, and nothing should be allowed to interfere with that. A good window treatment improves on a window's practical functions while greatly enhancing its decorative value. The right choice or combination of draperies, curtains, shades, or blinds can control the light, cut down the noise from outside, keep the room cooler in summer and warmer in winter, play up a beautiful view or hide an ugly one, conceal a window's defects or enhance its architectural value. At the same time it provides still another chance to use the magic properties of color, pattern, texture, and proportion in creating an effective decorating scheme.

Drapery and Curtain Headings

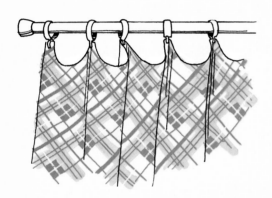

Scalloped café

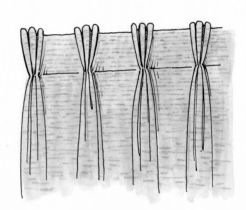

Pinch pleat

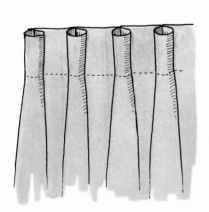

Cartridge pleat

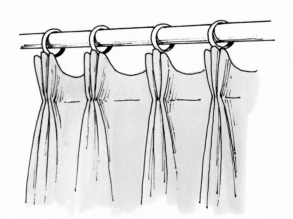

Pleated and scalloped

You have a choice of draperies, curtains, shades, or blinds, or a combination of two or more of the above, plus any number of valance or cornice designs to give them a crowning finish.

Draperies. When completely closed, draperies cover the window; when open, they frame it. They may be hung from the top of the window, somewhere above it, or at the ceiling line to reach the windowsill, apron, or floor. Their degree of formality depends on the fabric used as well as on additional decorative elements such as cornices, swags, jabots, and ties that can add eighteenth-century formality or be severely simple.

Curtains. Draperies are frequently hung with curtains behind them, closer to the window. Glass, or sash curtains, are usually made of sheer fabric to admit daylight while providing privacy.

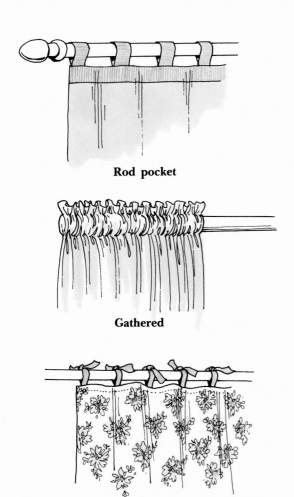

Rod pocket

Gathered

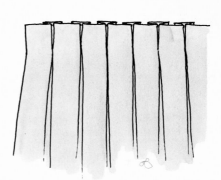

Box pleat

Tabs

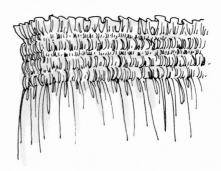

Shirred

Tiebacks

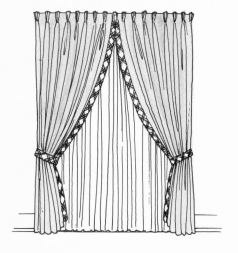

Low tiebacks

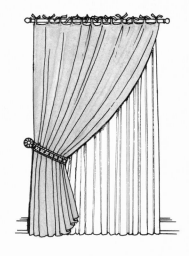

One-Way tieback

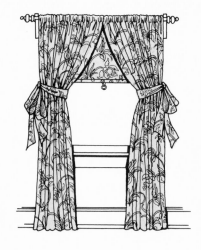

High tiebacks

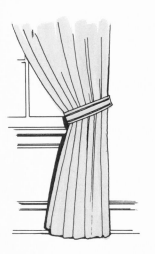

Tailored tieback

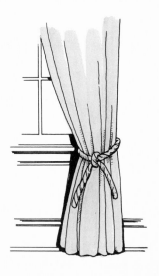

Silk Cord tieback

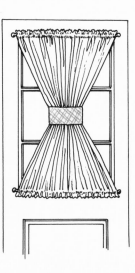

Hourglass tieback

Ruffled tieback

Double-Ruffled tieback

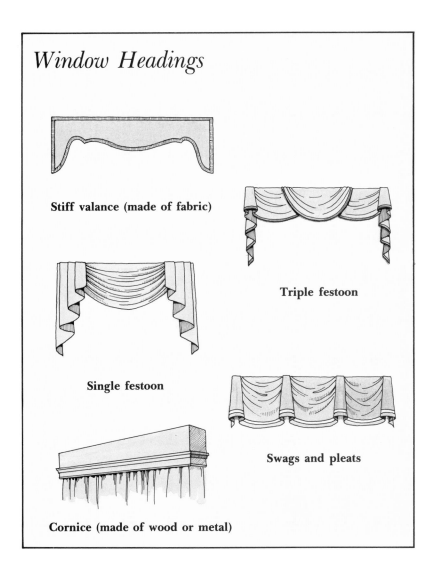

Window Headings

Stiff valance (made of fabric)

Triple festoon

Single festoon

Swags and pleats

Cornice (made of wood or metal)

They are hung on a stationary rod close to the window glass, and may extend to the sill, the apron, or the floor. Tailored curtains are always hung straight; ruffled curtains may be tied back straight to the sides or criss-crossed at the top and then tied back.

Casement curtains. Usually made of heavier fabric than glass curtains, casement curtains are also translucent, often with an open weave. They are hung from traverse rods that permit them to be drawn back for easy access to the cranks or handles that control the opening and closing of the windows. They, too, may extend to the sill, the apron, or the floor.

Café curtains. Traditionally hung with rings on café rods, café curtains may be in two overlapping tiers to cover the window completely or one tier that covers the lower half only, as in French cafés where they originated. Actually, the curtains may be finished with a variety of differently shaped headings and hung with different hardware on fabric tabs.

OPPOSITE PAGE:

Tied-back cottage curtains, topped by a shirred valance, create a simple, homey window treatment. Shelves placed within the frame hold dining and kitchen collectibles.

ABOVE:

Roll-up window shades may be made of any fabric firm yet light enough to function properly. The striped fabric used on the chair in the foreground and repeated at the window is a deft contrast to the horizontal pattern of the wall paneling.

LEFT:

Roman shades, like those in this informal bedroom, are the most tailored of all rollerless fabric window shades. As they are raised, they create a pleasing horizontal pattern. The striped fabric, which adds an illusion of height to the room, is repeated on the lounge chair in the foreground to unify the color scheme.

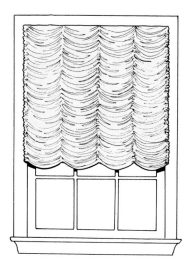

Austrian shade

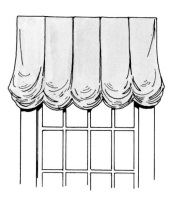

Inverted box shade

Shades, Blinds, and Shutters

Roller shades. The most familiar and simple of all shades, the roller variety, consists of laminated shade cloth and a roller around which it is wound. Roller-shade cloth is available in light-control densities from translucent (allowing the most daylight) to opaque (allowing no daylight). Such shades are made in a wide gamut of colors, fabrics, and patterns ranging from formal moiré to homespun effects. You can also buy a kit to make your own shade, using iron-on laminated shade cloth on your choice of fabric and attaching it to a roller that can be purchased separately.

Soft fabric shades. These rollerless shades are drawn up by means of a single cord attached to three or more cords, each of which runs through rings set in a tape stitched up the back of the shade; the tapes are spaced at even intervals. The three most popular types of soft fabric shades are Roman, Austrian, and balloon. Any of these shade types may be used with draperies, and all are dressier than most curtains. Again, their degree of formality depends on the fabric used.

Roman shades. The most tailored of the soft shade types, Roman shades draw up in even, flat panels that create a neat horizontal pattern. They require a medium-weight fabric that folds easily without being too heavy, and they should be lined.

Austrian shades. Much more formal and very soft in nature, Austrian shades are divided into vertical panels that are gathered with sheering tape into soft scallops from top to bottom. They require a lightweight fabric and are often made sheer for installation under draperies in a formal room.

Balloon shades. The fabric in balloon shades unfolds smoothly as it is lowered, giving the shade a somewhat tailored look, but

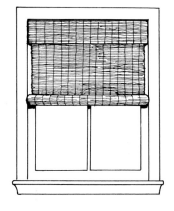

Matchstick blind

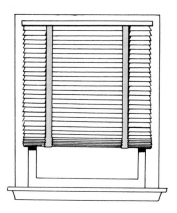

Venetian blind

the bottom always has a billowy scalloped edge and the shade draws up in scallops from the bottom as it is raised. This type of shade is best made in a medium-weight fabric with some body, and it should be lined.

Venetian blinds. Thomas Jefferson first brought venetian blinds to this country from Venice. Now they are made in a great variety of colors and slat widths, from narrow to wide, and in wood, metal, cloth, or plastic. They can also be hung either horizontally or vertically for complete control of light, air, and privacy. Venetian blinds can be used with curtains and/ or draperies, depending on the degree of formality you want to achieve.

Roll-up blinds. The materials used in making roll-up blinds include split bamboo, matchsticks, or wooden slats woven with yarn to add both color and texture. All three are pulled by cords that run from the bottom up, and they are available in readymade forms for standard-size windows or they can be custom-made to your specifications. Split-bamboo and wooden slats are wider and provide more privacy than the thinner matchstick type. Draperies and a cornice installed over the blinds add more formal finishing touches to blinds.

Shutters. Whether stationary or adjustable, louvered shutters add architectural interest when used to frame an otherwise ordinary window. Hinged shutter panels can also be used instead of curtains within a window frame—folded back for daylight and closed for nighttime privacy; draperies at either side can be added for formality. Unfinished shutters to be stained or painted are available from lumber dealers in both standard and custom sizes. Solid panel shutters and open frames in which gathered fabric can be inserted are also available. Staining is the more traditional method of finishing, and stain is much easier to apply than paint.

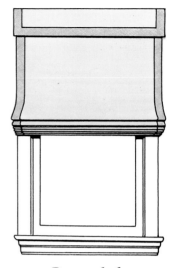

Roman shade

Balloon shade

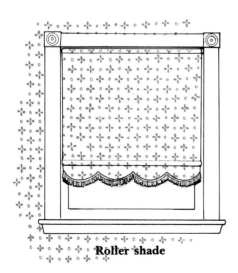

Roller shade

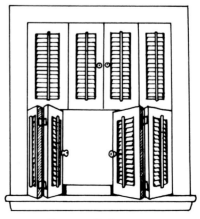

Louvered shutters

If window moldings provide a strong architectural effect that you want to maintain, and the windows are adequately recessed, tieback curtains hung within the window frame are a good solution.

Balloon shades have a billowy, scalloped bottom edge when raised but look tailored and smooth when lowered. They may be formal or informal, depending on the fabric chosen. The shades in this room repeat the wall-covering pattern but in a light color to admit more daylight.

Curtain and Drapery Hardware

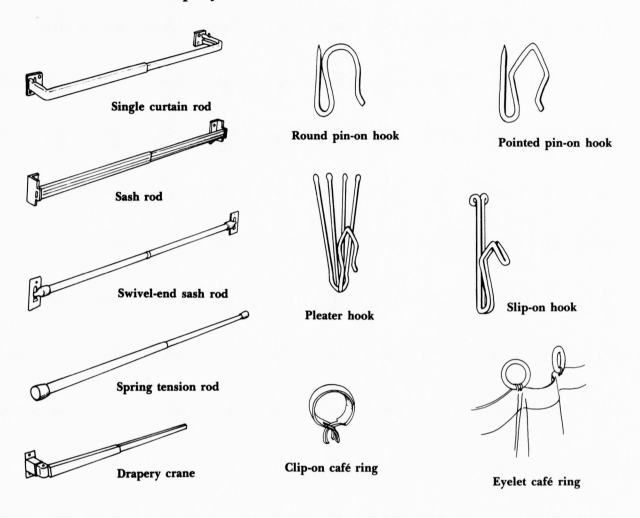

Single curtain rod

Sash rod

Swivel-end sash rod

Spring tension rod

Drapery crane

Round pin-on hook

Pointed pin-on hook

Pleater hook

Slip-on hook

Clip-on café ring

Eyelet café ring

Window Hardware

Specially designed rods, both functional and decorative, are available for every conceivable type of window treatment. Adjustable spring tension rods that fit tightly within the window frame require no installation: You simply adjust the rod to your window size and slip it into place. Rods of this type are particularly good for café curtains on rings or for those that have tabs, or a casing, or a pocket across the top.

Other functional single rods include hinged cranes used for swinging curtains away from inward-opening casement windows or french doors and traverse rods that draw draperies to either side of window or to one side only. Double-traverse rods let you draw back curtains and draperies separately; a triple-traverse rod is topped by a stationary curtain rod to hold a shirred valance.

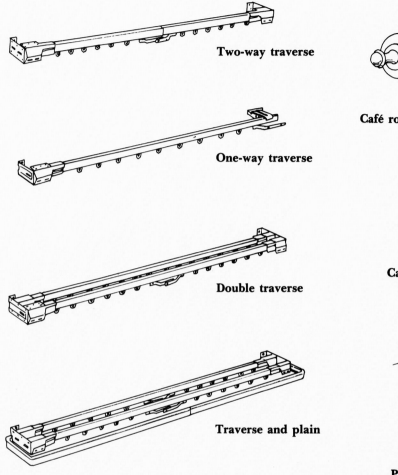

Two-way traverse

One-way traverse

Double traverse

Traverse and plain

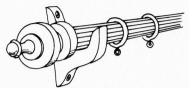

Café rod with arm support and rings

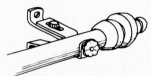

Café rod with support

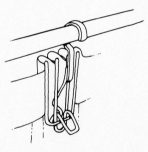

Pleater hook with ring

You will also find special rods designed for both bow and bay windows, ceiling mounted tracks for draw draperies—even rods that turn a right angle for corner windows. And, of course, there are drapery hooks specifically designed for use with the various types of rods.

Decorative rods are available in both metal and wood in a variety of colors and finishes for both café curtains and traverse designs with slides for attaching draw draperies that are suspended from hooks.

Hooks range from simple eyelit rings for cafés to pleater hooks for drapery.

The type of hardware you use and how you install it will influence the success of any window treatment. Within or outside the window casing is seldom a problem, but if you are using a rod on dry-wall construction, fasten it to studs for safer anchorage or on joists for ceiling rods.

Deciding on the Right Window Treatment

The choice of window treatment of any room should complement its overall decoration in terms of color, pattern, and texture. In addition, it should be compatible with the type of window being covered—never interfering with the mechanical operation of its opening and closing. Thinking and planning before buying can mean the difference between ordinary and effective window treatments.

Fabrics for curtains, draperies, and shades range from simple homespun and burlap to elegant velvets and brocades; patterns and colors are available in seemingly endless variety. Man-made fibers are woven to imitate the look of the more expensive natural fibers such as silk, wool, linen, or cotton, and the natural fibers are often blended with man-made fibers to create reasonably priced fabrics that have greater wearability and cleanability.

Always check hang tags or labels for fiber content and colorfastness, as well as for soil-resistant and permanent-press finishes. The terms *vat-dyed* or *solution-dyed* on labels indicate colorfastness, which is particularly important if the curtains will be exposed to strong sunlight. For longer wear, it is always advisable to line draperies as well as any of the soft shades made with a medium-weight fabric.

If your windows are standard in size, ready-made curtains and draperies are usually available, sometimes immediately, and they can create any mood from formal to casual. However, it is not always possible to get the fabric you want in ready-made curtains, which also are often skimpy-looking compared to their custom-made counterparts. You do have the advantage of seeing what they will look like in advance, however.

If you buy ready-mades, check to see that the bottom and side hems are neatly turned with blind stitching; bottom hems should be at least two inches deep; four or six is preferable but rare in ready-mades. The heading for draperies should be about four inches deep and backed to give body to the pleating.

At additional cost, curtains and draperies can be made to measure by a manufacturer or a drapery workroom. If you have curtains made and you do the measuring yourself, take accurate measurements with a wooden fold-out ruler and mark them on a sketch of each window that has individual specifications. Keep a copy for yourself and give the original to the store; otherwise you will have no recourse if the curtains don't fit. A drapery workroom will send someone to measure the windows. They will also hang the finished product, and will assume responsibility for the final fit.

Not all situations are ideal. Windows can be placed in an awkward location, or other factors may create a bewildering set of decorating problems. With the wide variety of treatments available, and with a good dose of imagination, you can resolve these problems. On the next pages you will find some of the more common situations, with recommendations for possible solutions.

How to Make the Most of Windows

■ If windows are framed by handsome moldings and you won't obstruct too much daylight, let the moldings be a decorative asset by mounting the curtain rods, if possible, within the casing. Conversely, if the molding is humdrum or nonexistent, mount the rods on the frame or beyond it on the wall.

■ If you have a view of a neighboring building, use a treatment that admits light but blocks the view during the day—perhaps gauzy glass curtains—supplemented by heavier draw draperies for privacy at night.

■ If a room gets too much sunlight during the day, control the glaring light and summer heat, again with a glass curtain or with sheer shades or blinds augmented by draperies.

■ City noise can be muffled or reduced by heavy, lined draperies.

■ Awkwardly placed windows can be made part of an entire curtained wall by arranging a traverse rod to draw curtains or draperies away from the window area only during the daytime, leaving the rest of the wall covered.

■ Clerestory windows high on a wall are designed to let in light *and* maintain privacy; they need not be curtained unless they are in a bedroom where early morning light could be a problem.

OPPOSITE PAGE:

Tall casement windows in the generously sized bay window area of a vintage house are left uncurtained for a view only partly screened by tall plants. The furniture, including the child's high chair, is early twentieth century in style.

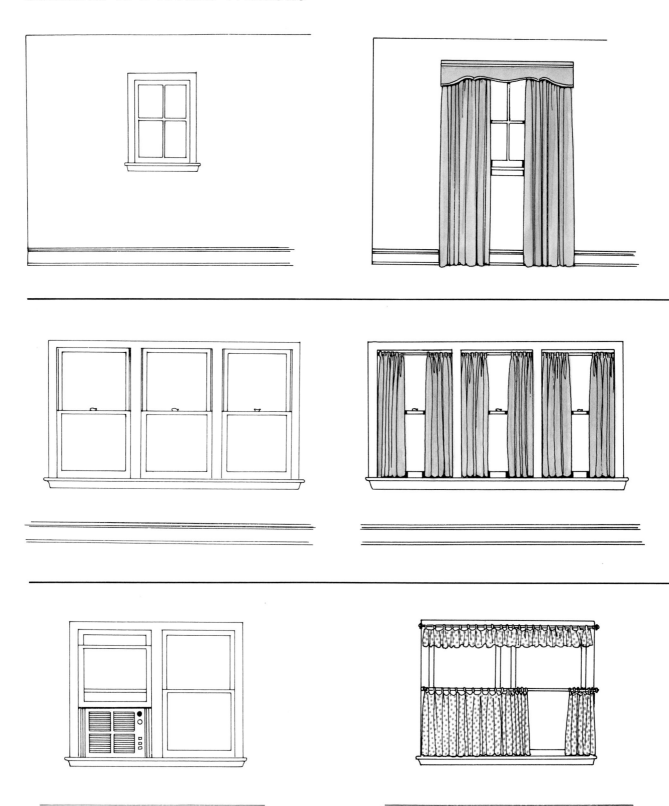

PROBLEM A small and insignificant double-hung window that is out of scale with the surrounding wall area.

SOLUTION 1 Add importance with floor-to-ceiling draperies on a rod that extends well beyond the window frame; hide the drapery fixture with a graceful cornice.

SOLUTION 2 For an informal look, gain width and size by adding hinged shutters that can be opened to admit daylight and closed across the window for nighttime privacy.

PROBLEM Adding distinction to three adjoining double-hung windows that dominate a room.

SOLUTION 1 For an informal look, each window can be treated individually with full-length café curtains.

SOLUTION 2 For a more formal effect, and to unify the windows, use floor-length tie-back draperies with rods that extend beyond the window area; and a roller shade underneath that covers all three.

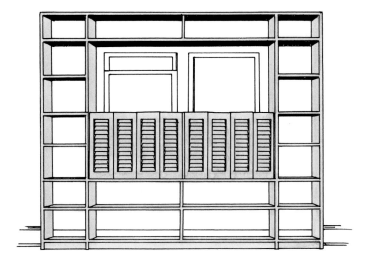

PROBLEM Concealing the air conditioner in a window.

SOLUTION 1 For an informal and cohesive look, use café curtains and a valance—both on single rods—in a fabric that matches the wall covering to further camouflage the machine.

SOLUTION 2 Add architectural interest to the entire wall by using louvered shutters on the lower half of both windows, and surrounding them with bookcases to hold a display of treasures, in addition to books.

PROBLEM A pair of windows that turns a corner admits too much glaring sunlight or looks out on an ugly view.

SOLUTION 1 Sunlight as well as the view can be controlled by hanging floor-length sheer glass curtains under heavy draperies on a double traverse rod over both windows.

SOLUTION 2 For a softer, elegant look, an Austrian shade on each window is also effective. Roman shades or blinds would also work well.

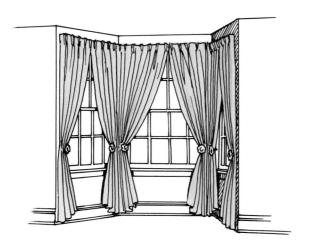

PROBLEM Adding privacy to a bay window that looks out on the street.

SOLUTION 1 Use a single tier of café curtains on the lower half of the windows to shield that portion alone from view or a double tier of curtains to provide complete privacy. Creating a window seat in the space will add storage under the seat as well as a cozy place to sit.

SOLUTION 2 For an open bay area, floor-length draperies can be tied back during the daytime, closed at night.

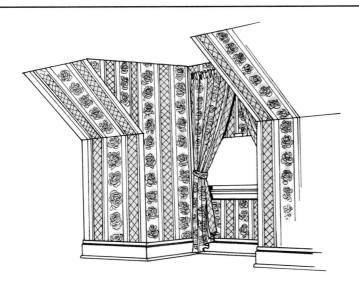

PROBLEM Decorating around double-hung dormer windows.

SOLUTION 1 Place utilitarian cabinetry in the space beneath the window and achieve a simple, but finished effect with a contour-edged window shade.

SOLUTION 2 To camouflage both the window and sloping walls, use the same pattern for tie-back draperies and wall covering. A vertical design will add height to the walls.

Solutions to French Doors

Calculating Fabric for Draperies or Curtains

Be sure to take accurate measurements with a wooden fold-out ruler and mark them on a sketch of each different window.

Width. For draperies meant to meet in the center, the unpleated width (measured across the top), should be two and a half or three times the window width (three for very sheer fabric), plus at least 19 to 22 inches (allowing for a 3- or 4-inch overlap at the point of closure), plus 8 to 10 inches to cover the right-angle turns at each end of the rod, and 8 inches for 1-inch double hems at both sides of each completed panel.

In addition, you need to figure out how much beyond the window you want the curtains or draperies to extend when drawn open so as not to block out the light. When drawn open just to the window frame, pleated fabric will cover one third of the window area. Generally you will want to overlap the window by no more than 3 inches to 7 inches on each side. Decide what you want the total overlap (both sides) to be and subtract that amount from one-third of the window width. Add the remainder to the fabric width determined earlier. (Example: If a window is 6 feet wide, 2 feet, or 24 inches, will be

PROBLEM French doors are needed for daylight but must often be curtained for privacy.

SOLUTION 1 Panels of sheer fabric, shirred on rods attached to the doors, will admit diffused daylight but provide privacy at night; the top panes are left open for a view.

SOLUTION 2 For a more formal effect, draw draperies installed on a traverse rod wider than the doors and hidden by a cornice, can be closed for night-time privacy.

covered if the draperies are drawn just to the window frame. If you only want to cover 3 inches on each side, subtract a total of 6 inches from 24 inches, and add the remainder, or 18 inches, to the previously determined width of the fabric. The curtain rod must then extend 9 inches beyond the inner edge at each side of the frame.) Finally, to determine the number of panels you will need to make the curtains or draperies, divide the total width just determined by the width of your fabric.

Length and total fabric required. Floor-length draperies should hang about a half-inch above the floor or carpet. For full-length draperies or curtains, add 14 or 16 inches to the desired length to allow for 3-inch doubled headings (for pinch pleats) and double 4-inch hems at the bottom. Add two more inches for a shaped heading. For curtains or draperies that will hang to the sill, allow for only 3-inch double hems.

If you are using fabric that has a pattern repeat, also add the length of the repeat to the total length you have just calculated for each panel. Then, to determine the total amount of fabric you will need, multiply that length by the number of panels you arrived at under "width" and divide by 36 to get the total yards of fabric required.

How to Measure
a Window

WIDTH, DEPENDING ON THE TREATMENT
DESIRED:

■ **Measure from one end of the rod to
the other, excluding the bent ends (or
returns), if any. (A)**

■ **Measure the top of the window
frame, from one outside edge to the
other. (B)**

■ **Measure inside the window frame
from one jamb to the other. (C)**

LENGTH, DEPENDING ON THE TREATMENT
DESIRED: *

■ **Measure from the top of the window
frame, or rod, to the floor. (D)**

■ **Measure from the top of the window
frame, or rod, to the bottom of the sill.
(E)**

■ **Measure from the top of the window
frame, or rod, to the top of the sill. (F)**

■ **Measure from the top of the sash to
the top of the sill. (G)**

Note: If you are planning to use rods
with rings from which the draperies or
curtains will hang, measure from the
bottom of the rings.

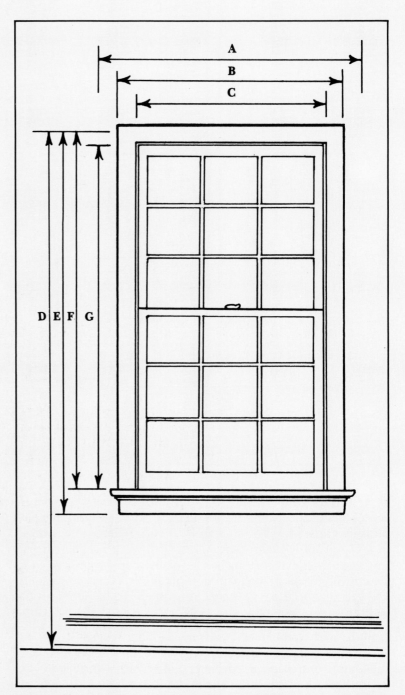

Hinged louvered shutters, instead of curtains or draperies, add architectural interest when used to frame otherwise ordinary windows; they may be folded back during the daytime and closed over the windows for nighttime privacy. In this bedroom, designed to grow with a young girl, reproduction furniture is in the best early American spirit.

CHAPTER TEN

Lighting your home

Although Benjamin Franklin—with his kite in hand—is often credited with discovering electricity, it was Thomas Edison and his light bulb who showed us what to do with it. Before this comparatively recent invention in lighting, our ancestors progressed slowly and dimly from fire and candlelight through whale oil and kerosene lamps to the mid-nineteenth-century miracle of gaslight. Today we can have as much light as we want in any quantity—brilliant, subdued, or in between— exactly where we want it and from both decorative and functional sources.

Never underestimate the importance of light in any decorative scheme. Light makes colors come alive; color, in turn, affects the quantity and quality of light. White and pale hues reflect most of the light that reaches them, making a room look brighter. Deep hues absorb light, increasing the amount of illumination needed. You have probably noticed too how light borrows color from a surface that reflects it. In a room with a green rug and green draperies, the light itself seems to have a verdant cast to it, like light under the trees in summer.

Because artificial lighting can be planned and controlled, most rooms are every bit as attractive by night as by day. Thinking of lighting in this way, as a decorating tool as well as a practical necessity, will help you make the most effective use of it.

OPPOSITE PAGE:

Dining tables, wherever they may be, are best lighted by a fixture hanging directly over the table; a dimmer switch makes it possible to control the amount of light from dim to bright. This reproduction of a late-Colonial brass chandelier adds a touch of elegance to the country-look room.

Lamps and Shade Heights

■ A table lamp should be 39 to 42 inches from the bottom of the shade to the floor.

■ A desk lamp should be 15 inches from the base of the lamp to the bottom of the shade.

■ A bedside lamp should be about 20 inches from the top of the mattress to the bottom of the shade.

■ A lamp shade should be deep enough to shield the eyes from the bulb, whether you are sitting or standing.

■ If the shade of a tall lamp extends below the recommended level, use a translucent shade that allows more light to penetrate through it.

Planning a Lighting Scheme

You have a choice of three basic sources of artificial light—portable lamps to move about as you please, permanently installed fixtures and architectural lighting elements such as an illuminated wall or ceiling panel, or spot or strip lighting of various types. Fortunately for those of us who prefer traditional decorating, the best designs in both fixtures and portable lamps have survived the test of generations and can be found in every form from candlestick to chandelier.

Every room needs some form of background lighting—diffused and soft—as opposed to the direct light needed for reading, sewing, cooking, or anything that requires eye concentration; direct light of this type is usually obtained from portable lamps in living rooms, bedrooms, or family rooms and from architectural lighting in kitchens and bathrooms.

Consider Each Room

In planning a lighting scheme, think about the purpose each room serves. In a living room or family room, where everyone gathers for conversation or games and for parties large or small, lighting should be well diffused and at a fairly high level of intensity; for an average-size room you will need a minimum of five lamps or an equivalent combination of fixtures and lamps. The intensity of the light—bright for large gatherings, dimmer for more intimate groups—can be controlled by using lamps with three-way bulbs and switches and by installing dimmer systems for fixtures.

Dining tables, whether in a separate room or an area of a living room, family room, or kitchen, are best lighted by a fixture hanging directly over the table. In a formal dining room, wall sconces soften and add to general illumination. Again, a dimmer system makes it possible to control, separately, the sconces and chandelier—average light for informal meals; dim and combined with candlelight for formal dinners.

If you plan your lighting for reading, bear in mind these standards: The average eye level of a seated person is 38 to 42 inches above the floor, so a table lamp—placed next to a sofa or chair—should be 38 to 42 inches from the bottom of the shade to the floor. A floor lamp should be 42 to 49 inches from the floor to the bottom of the shade. For reading comfort, you should place a floor lamp close to the right or left rear corner of the chair, a placement that is possible only when chairs or sofas are at least 10 to 12 inches from the wall. A desk lamp should be about 15 inches from the base of the lamp to the bottom of the shade. A bedside lamp should be about 20 inches from the top of the mattress to the bottom of the shade, and hanging light fixtures should be 58 to 63 inches from the floor.

Bedroom lighting can be planned to suit individual needs. A

bedside lamp or wall-hung fixture should provide adequate light for reading. (Lamps with a switch on the cord or base are easier to reach while dozing off.) Dresser and dressing table mirrors should have lamps on either side to light the face evenly; white translucent shades and warm white bulbs are best for an undistorted reflection of skin tones.

Lighting in rooms for small children should be planned for safety. Place lamps well out of a child's reach to avoid the risk of their being knocked over or of the child's touching a hot bulb. Wall fixtures should be firmly attached and also out of the child's reach.

In areas used for sewing, concentrated study, or extended reading, strong lighting is needed. A pair of lamps (preferably equipped with diffusing bowls) or well-placed wall-mounted fixtures is the absolute minimum.

Another way to light these areas is to mount fluorescent strips on the wall or under a shelf. Strip lighting is excellent for sewing if your machine is in a fixed location. If you have a portable machine, place it in the best position for general overall lighting and focus the light of a floor or table lamp on it.

More general work areas, such as kitchens, laundry rooms, workshops, or hobby rooms (as well as bathrooms), require ample overall lighting, without shadows, for convenience and safety. Ideally, a kitchen should have several ceiling lights or a completely luminous ceiling, supplemented by additional lighting in food-preparation areas. Here again strip units are extremely useful; installed beneath wall-hung cupboards, they flood the work areas below with light. Bathroom mirrors should have fixtures on both sides or strip lighting surrounding the mirror. General illumination can be provided by a ceiling fixture, wall sconces, or baffled fluorescent strip lighting. The same principle of good general lighting, plus concentrated illumination in special areas, should be applied to any room used primarily for work, whatever its nature.

A fanciful Victorian fixture lights the dining area in this cheerful family room. Pressed-back dining chairs of this type were machine made during the late nineteenth and early twentieth centuries. Because of our great interest in nostalgic furnishings, the style has been revived and is again being made.

Fluorescent Versus Incandescent Lighting

For work areas where a high level of illumination is required, fluorescent lighting is recommended, not only because it creates less surface heat but because it is cheaper to operate and lasts longer than incandescent lighting. For other areas the choice is a matter of personal preference. Light from fluorescent tubes ranges from warm to cool. Because it causes less color distortion, warm white is best for home use; cool white is unflattering to food and skin tones, and it tends to gray or deaden most colors. Generally speaking, the incandescent bulbs used in portable lamps cast a warmer light and cause less distortion of color. And, thanks to a recent invention, you can now get the same warm effect with circular fluorescent tubes that fit most lamps.

OPPOSITE PAGE:

Track lighting over the double sink in this kitchen highlights copper pots hanging from a butcher's rack and adds sparkle to early apothecary jars displayed behind the sink. An antique double fixture lights a work area under the window; general illumination is provided by the multiple units of fixtures converted from kerosene to electricity.

BELOW:

For our early ancestors, lighting was limited to homemade candles and firelight. This wrought-iron chandelier has a centrally located glass ball to reflect further light from its four candles; wall sconces above the chest are also equipped with reflectors. The wrought-iron double candleholder on the right is the ancestor of present-day floor lamps.

Lamp Styles

Jar

Vase

Canister

Victorian parlor

Student

What to Look for in Lamps

In addition to the light they provide, lamps are decorative features in a room, serving as lively accessories. When selecting a lamp for a specific task, consider the quantity and quality of the light required, the location of the lamp, and the suitability of its shape, size, and color in the room.

Portable lamps are available in a great variety of classic traditional styles, from elegant to simple. In addition to style, the materials used for base and shade also affect the degree of formality; a porcelain jar-shaped lamp with a silk shade is far

Column

Ginger jar

Candlestick

Punctured tin

Tiffany

Triple candlestick

more elegant than a similar base made of ironstone with a printed linen shade. Classic traditional formal shapes include candlestick, column, ginger jar, cylinder, and vase; less formal styles include reproductions of nineteenth-century oil lamps in tole, pewter, or brass, as well as ceramic jugs, crocks, or jars and metal canisters.

The inside of every shade should be flat white or only slightly tinted to maximize the amount of light that will be reflected from it. The outside color of the shade looks best when it harmonizes with the walls and furnishings; a neutral, translucent shade will cast the most light.

Formal lamps usually have shades made of parchment or silk in white or colors or of enameled or marbelized paper. Informal lamp shades may be of patterned or solid-color cloth or paper, metal, or glass (which is often used for reproductions of oil lamps). Translucent shades allow more light into a room, appearing as bright areas and adding to the overall illumination. Opaque shades aim the light up and down and are helpful in toning down a room with a high level of light reflected from architectural sources.

Style and Scale

In choosing a lamp, make sure it suits the degree of formality that you want to achieve; then check the size and shape to be sure that it will be compatible with the table, desk, dresser, or wherever you plan to use it. The shade width should also be in proper proportion to the base and should never exceed the width of the tabletop; a large lamp will look ridiculous on a small table, and a small lamp will be lost on a large surface.

Portable lamps are available in great variety from elegantly formal to deep-country casual. Here, an old jug has been electrified and given an informal shade of checked linen.

In a city apartment furnished country style, a primitive early-Colonial-style chandelier lights the foyer. The quilt's geometric design accentuates the stencil design added to the herringbone pattern of the floor.

CHAPTER ELEVEN

Traditional table settings

Table settings offer, each day, a fresh chance to add beauty and interest to your home, and they are an excellent means of enhancing the traditional style of your home. They can also make every meal an occasion, whether it's a simple breakfast served on placemats or a formal dinner gleaming with crystal and silver. The important ingredient is imagination combined with knowledgeable attention to traditional designs, and the necessary tools are carefully selected dinnerware, glasses, flatware, and table coverings.

The Early American Table

The earliest American tables were set, chiefly, with pewter plates, tankards, mugs, tureens, spoons, knives, and forks—all imported from England. Those who could not afford pewter used wooden plates, cups, and bowls, called *treenware* because of its tree source, or simple earthenware made by local potters. Colonial pewter was first made in Boston in the 1640s and, as more craftsmen emigrated to the colonies, it became generally available by the eighteenth century.

Colonial silversmiths were active as early as 1650 in New England and in New York. Our colonial craftsmen were extremely active in church and civic affairs and well-respected members of their communities. (Paul Revere, our most famous colonial silversmith, left a legacy of beautifully simple patterns

OPPOSITE PAGE:

Centerpieces offer an unlimited opportunity to be creative in thinking of new uses for things you already own. Here, a carefully sliced watermelon—both decorative and edible—is perched on a toy wagon, adding bright color to an informal luncheon. The casual window treatment combines roll-up matchstick blinds with boldly patterned draperies.

Traditional Table Settings

Flatware should be set in order of use, working from the outside toward the plate. The formal dinner setting shows a soup spoon for the first course on the far right; forks on the left will be used for a second course salad, for the main course, and for dessert. Knives should always be placed with the cutting edge toward the plate. Water glasses go directly above the knife; wine glasses and breakfast juice glasses are placed to the right of the water glass. Folded napkins may be placed to the left of the fork or directly on the plate.

Breakfast

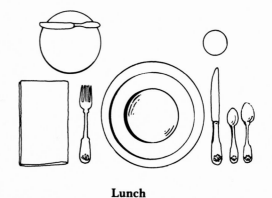

Lunch

Informal Dinner

Formal Dinner

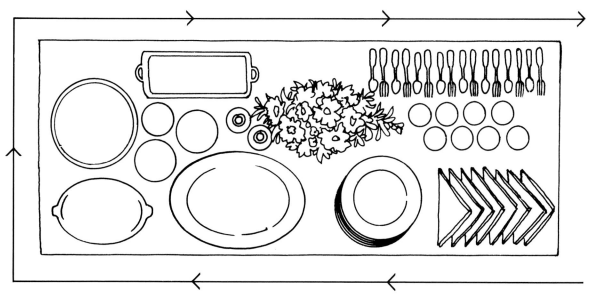

that are still being made today.) Most early silver was made of melted English coins alloyed with copper for strength. Lacking any sort of banking facility for depositing surplus money, wealthy colonists commissioned local silversmiths to convert their extra money into household goods. Unlike the registered English guild hall marks that stamp each sterling piece with the maker's mark and the date, American silversmiths stamped their work with their names or initials as a guarantee of the integrity of their coin silver.

Only the wealthy could possibly afford silver; so pewter remained the tableware of the middle class until about 1765, when it began to wane in popularity.

The first American pottery, established in Jamestown in 1610, turned out simple earthenware for kitchen and table use. By 1685 potters in New York, Massachusetts, Maryland, Pennsylvania, and Virginia were producing household wares modeled on imports from factories in Staffordshire. Early pieces were usually made of lead-glazed red clay or salt-glazed stoneware. There was very little production of fine pottery before the Revolution.

American China

The generic term *china* harks back to the time when fine porcelain was imported to European countries from China. European ceramists were unable to duplicate the nonporous translucent import until the turn of the eighteenth century when two Germans discovered the combination of kaolin clay and feldspar, fired at extremely high temperatures, that produces porcelain. Soon thereafter, factories were established at Meissen and Dresden to turn out the European version of chinaware. Potters in England added bone ash to their clays to create a translucent bone china that is still made today.

A Buffet Setting

This table is set to allow traffic to move easily around it. Guests first pick up a napkin and plate, serve themselves to food, and, finally, pick up a wine glass and flatware. If you have many guests, and the table is large enough, buffet service can be expedited by setting up separate traffic lanes at each end of the table and placing double servings of food in the middle.

If the table is set against a wall, move the centerpiece and candles back toward the wall to allow more room for food service in the center of the table. Napkins and plates can then be placed on the right, wine glasses and flatware on the left.

Porcelain was first made in America by William Ellis Tucker, who turned out quantities of fine dinnerware in Philadelphia from 1826 until 1832. Tucker's translucent white china was decorated with gold in imitation of the French Sevres ware, but because Americans thought French china superior, his ware is mostly unmarked.

Today, fine china is made of refined clays fired at much higher temperatures than other types of dinnerware. Except for gold, silver, or platinum, decoration is applied, either by hand or by a transfer method, before the piece is sprayed with or dipped in a ceramic glaze that may be clear or add color to the body. A final firing fuses the glaze to the clay body, protecting the decoration with a tough, glasslike coating.

Fine china is usually sold by the place setting. A three-piece buffet setting consists of a dinner plate and a cup and saucer; salad and bread-and-butter plates are included in a five-piece setting; a six-piece set includes a soup cup or plate. Serving pieces are usually made to match most china patterns, or you may add variety and contrast by using other pieces, such as a pewter tureen, a glass or wooden salad bowl, a silver platter, or an earthenware vegetable dish.

Stores usually have a display of "open stock" fine china patterns, which means that additional pieces may be bought as long as the store stocks the pattern and the manufacturer continues to make it. Some of the classic patterns in fine china have been in continuous production since the eighteenth century and will likely stay in stock as long as the demand for traditional styles continues. But these patterns are the exception, and you can't always count on being able to replace broken pieces of other patterns after a year or more.

Earthenware

Earthenware is made of less refined clays fired at lower temperatures; the body is more porous and less resistant to cracking and chipping than fine china. Sometimes called pottery, earthenware varies in thickness from hard-bodied stoneware or ironstone to the thickness of fine china without its translucence.

Like fine china, earthenware is made in a great variety of patterns, including reproductions of early spongeware and slipware. Earthenware is usually sold in sets—service for four, six, eight, and sometimes twelve—and is less expensive than fine china. If your budget limits you to one set of dinnerware, choose a simple undecorated shape, perhaps of sturdy white ironstone, that can be used for any occasion.

Selecting Flatware

The general term designated for knives, forks, spoons, ladles, and other table utensils, flatware is made in sterling or silver plate, pewter, stainless steel, and vermeil. Traditional patterns range from simple early colonial to rococo baroque.

Sterling silver. Sterling silver flatware made today is 85.2 percent pure silver with copper added for strength. It is sometimes sold in sets, but it is more often bought by the place setting or by individual pieces. Silver plate is made by electroplating a coating of silver on a base metal, and the thicker the coating of silver is, the longer it will wear. Sterling can be used daily for centuries without a sign of wear. The accumulated scratches it receives as it is used endow it with a soft and valued sheen called patina. Most silver plate gives at least one or more generations of use and can be replated if the base metal begins to show through on wear spots, such as the back of a spoon bowl. It is usually sold in sets and is less costly than sterling; prices vary depending on design and the thickness of the silver plate.

Silver does require polishing now and then; the very act of rubbing it adds to its patina. Always use a silver polish, never a dip that will leave your silver looking dull and lifeless, and always use a soft, nonabrasive cloth. The need for polishing sterling or silver plate is minimized by using it every day. Seldom-used pieces are best stored in specially treated cloth that helps to prevent tarnishing.

Pewter. Traditionally an alloy of tin and lead, pewter is now made without lead, but it still has the same familiar dull sheen of early pewter. Traditionalists find colonial patterns particularly appealing in pewter, which can be bought in sets or individual pieces. Prices vary, depending on design and weight.

Stainless steel. The widest quality range of flatware, from inexpensive lightweight to heavy pieces with the sheen of silver, are available in stainless steel. It is sold in sets or by the place setting.

Vermeil. Originally made of sterling silver plated with gold, vermeil no longer carries an astronomical price tag because gold is now applied to other metals. Less expensive facsimiles are also available.

Hollow ware. Serving dishes, trays, and table accessories such as candlesticks, salts and peppers, and sauceboats are made in sterling, silver plate, pewter, and stainless steel. Unlike flatware patterns, stainless steel hollow ware is most often modern in design. Both traditional and contemporary hollow ware designs are available in all the other materials, however.

Glassware

Attractive glassware makes a table sparkle; it is available in every price range. Tumblers or footed tumblers for water, juice, and iced tea are usually used for family meals and

Dining outdoors can be as informal as a picnic out of a hamper or as formal as this breakfast table set in a gazebo overlooking a river. Floral-patterned fine china repeats the theme of the table covering; plaid napkins contrast brightly with the floral patterns but complement the color scheme. The simple, classic shape of the silver is reminiscent of traditional bone or porcelain-handled table service. A blue blaze of cornflowers makes a brilliant centerpiece.

informal entertaining, while stemware (water goblet, sherbet/champagne glass, and an all-purpose wine glass or separate red and white wine glasses) is traditional for formal occasions. Cocktails, aperitifs, brandies, and liqueurs call for various special glasses. Individual glass finger bowls (usable for salads and desserts), glass dessert plates, and glass accessories such as salts and peppers, a water pitcher, and a salad bowl are also nice to have.

When shopping for glassware, you'll be confronted by a maze of terms. A few basic facts, to clear up confusion, follow.

Crystal. Also called lead crystal, crystal is the finest quality glass to which lead oxide has been added for brilliance and sparkle. Crystal is made in a variety of weights from stemware as delicate as a bubble to very heavy tumblers, candlesticks, pitchers, and vases.

Hand-blown crystal. Skilled craftsmen hand blow crystal by placing a blob of molten glass on the end of a hollow metal pipe and then turning the pipe while blowing through it to create the desired shape in the glass. The finest stemware and decorative glassware is hand blown.

Pressed glass. Made by pouring molten glass into a mold that is powered either by hand or by machine, pressed-glass patterns range from simple to elegant and elaborate. Color is added to the molten glass in the form of small amounts of metal oxide—cobalt for blue, iron for amber, copper for green. Opaque milk glass is made in colors as well as in white.

Cut glass. By holding the plain glass, or blank, shape to be decorated against revolving abrasive wheels, the sculptured designs of art glass are created. Engraving or etching is done with a pencil like tool that applies abrasive to the surface only. Because of the handwork involved, cut glass has more clarity and brilliance than the pressed variety and, of course, it costs more.

Table Coverings

Table coverings run the gamut from simple placemats of printed cotton or of straw to extremely formal double-damask tablecloths with matching napkins. In between these two extremes you will find a rainbow of colors and a plethora of patterns. There are no hard-and-fast rules for choosing table coverings and napkins—organdy placemats can be as formal as a damask tablecloth and, except for formal dinners, the napkins need not necessarily match the table covering. If the placemats or tablecloth are patterned, the napkins could be in the predominate color or in as many different colors as the pattern offers. If your china is boldly patterned, it is appropriate to select a cloth or mats in a solid color that matches or relates to the predominate or subordinate colors of your china;

OPPOSITE PAGE:

In a traditional dining room furnished with antiques, fine silver, china, and crystal are displayed against beautiful bare wood. A crystal chandelier, branched candelabra, and candles in hurricane shades throw a softly flattering light through the room.

napkins may be matching, contrasting, or all-purpose white.

If your tabletop is exceptionally attractive you may not want to cover it with anything; however, do protect the surface with service plates of china, pewter, or glass, and use trivets under hot serving dishes. Usually, it is still best to at least use placemats for a more finished look.

If you use a tablecloth, it should go over a pad and hang down from 12 to 16 inches below the tabletop. Dinner napkins should be 18 to 24 inches square; luncheon napkins may be smaller. Cloth napkins should be used for all but the most casual meals.

Centerpieces

Centerpieces add charm and interest to any meal from breakfast through dinner to a late supper. They may be purely decorative, such as a beautiful arrangement of flowers, or decorative and functional, such as a bowl of fruit to serve as the dessert course. A beautiful flowering houseplant or one with interesting foliage in an attractive cachepot makes an attractive centerpiece that can last for weeks. Handsome vegetables arranged on a tray or in a basket also make an attractive and colorful centerpiece for an informal dinner. Try mixing colors and shapes, such as cauliflower, eggplant, and squash, or do an all-green arrangement of broccoli, cucumbers, peppers, and curly endive.

Try to avoid the monotony of the expected and substitute variety with unexpected containers for your floral arrangements. Instead of the usual bowl or vase, use a pretty pitcher, cannister, or wine cooler for an arrangement of garden flowers. And don't overlook the beauty of blooming weeds like goldenrod, wild asters, and daisies. Let your imagination run wild, but try to make the mood of your centerpiece relate to your table setting, formal or casual.

Wherever your centerpiece fancy leads you, keep its height below the eye level of seated diners. And candlesticks should be either high enough or low enough to keep candle flames above or below eye level.

OPPOSITE PAGE ABOVE:

In a formal eighteenth-century dining room, a beautifully set table continues the theme established by lavish Christmas decorations on both sideboards and around the mantel. A red-and-white striped runner over a lace tablecloth, ribbon decorated napkins and floral centerpieces, massive twin candelabra, and silver service plates under fine china—all proclaim unrestrained holiday elegance.

OPPOSITE PAGE BELOW:

Fringed placemats of thick homespun linen protect the tabletop and provide a textured background for china color-keyed to the blue upholstery fabric and matching roman window shades. Similar, but not matching, candlesticks and a vivid centerpiece of daffodils add charm and interest to this luncheon table.

CHAPTER TWELVE

Kitchen and bath designs

Planning for the kitchen and bath presents special problems that deserve particular attention.

Kitchen Planning

While cooking activity is no longer centered around the hearth, and modern appliances have simplified and minimized both food preparation and cleanup, we still want our kitchens to be more than purely functional. We prefer a warm and friendly room with a cozy place to eat breakfast, as well as a place to display our treasures.

Only if you are building a new house or remodeling an old one will you face major problems, in which case it's advisable to take advantage of the professional kitchen-planning services offered by many contractors and appliance dealers. Many attractive variations are possible, depending on the space available and the amount of money you have to spend.

If you are planning a kitchen from scratch, you should be influenced by the amount of counter space generally required for the work area around the stove, sink, and refrigerator; the sizes of sink and appliances you have or want; and the room you like to have for the way you cook. Much research has been done on kitchens, and the information is available in special books on the subject.

OPPOSITE PAGE:

Brick floors and natural-wood cabinets preserve the traditional look of this kitchen. The white-tiled counter surrounding the sink is easy to maintain and helps to counterbalance the dark wood and the floor. A commodious antique cabinet on the right is ideal for kitchen storage, and the old table at the center of the room serves as extra work space.

Study the six floor plans illustrated here. Five contain a "work triangle" that indicates the pattern of movement between sink, stove, and refrigerator. A good rule of thumb to follow is that the sum of the lengths of the sides of the triangle should not exceed 21 feet. A few other rules should be considered as well. When the refrigerator door is open, it shouldn't interfere with the work triangle or with traffic into and out of the kitchen. The dishwasher should be installed near the sink

Basic Kitchen Plans

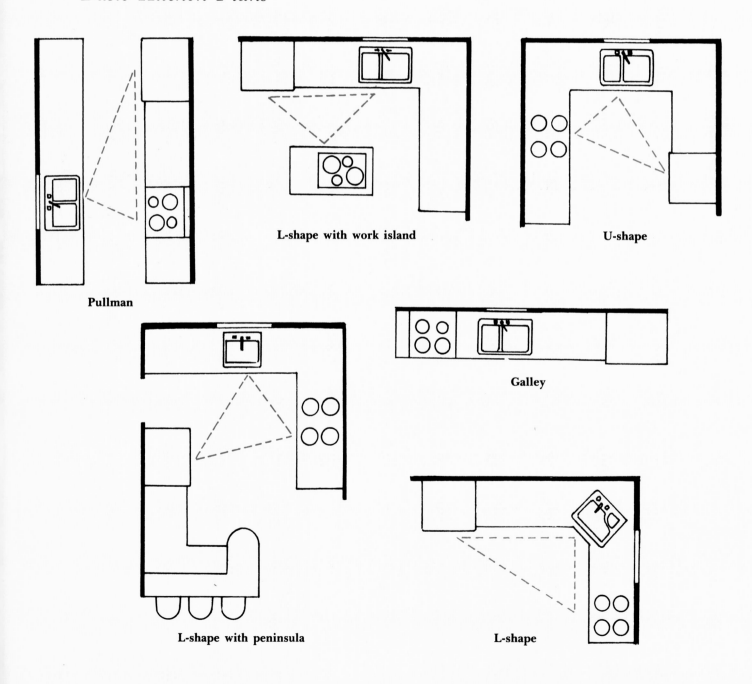

Pullman

L-shape with work island

U-shape

Galley

L-shape with peninsula

L-shape

but where it won't block access to the sink during loading. If the refrigerator can be located near the service entrance, so much the better. Since the sink area in a kitchen is used the most often, the sink should be centrally located within the work triangle, between the range and refrigerator. The oven, however, is the least used appliance, and so if you want to have built-in separate ovens, they need not be considered as part of the work triangle.

Liberal counter space is essential on both sides of the sink for cleanup after meals; allow 36 inches for stacking dishes prior to washing and, unless you have a dishwasher, 30 inches for draining. For setting out serving dishes or dinner plates, allow 24 inches of counter space on one side of the range or built-in stove unit. Ideally, there should be a minimum of 18 inches on each side of a stove. At least 18 inches of space is also needed at one side of the refrigerator for convenience in loading and unloading foods. When buying a refrigerator, you will have a choice of a right- or left-hinged door; the door should open *away* from the nearby counter space so as not to obstruct it when open. In larger rooms, additional counter and work space can be gained by adding an island or a peninsula with a built-in stove top or a sink surrounded by counter space.

Counter tops may be covered with plasic laminate, now available in wood grain, slate, and other natural looks, as well

In this compact U-shaped kitchen, sink, stove, and refrigerator are within easy reach of each other; the butcher block table serves as a work island. A cheerful clutter of working collectibles is carefully controlled: pots and pans hang from the rafters; an old double-wheeled coffee grinder serves its original purpose; utensils hang from hooks on the butcher block. More useful collectibles fill glass shelves at the window.

ABOVE:

This generous work island includes quantities of storage space and a second sink for the preparation of salads and vegetables (the main sink is located out of the photograph, to the left). Rough-sawn cedar paneling and custom cabinets are stained to the same warm glow, tieing the whole kitchen together; the white door pulls repeat the white of glazed terra-cotta tiles used on counter tops and behind the built-in stove. Wall space within the work area is put to maximum use with storage above the ovens and refrigerator; even the top of the hood is called into service. An antique rack, below the wall-hung copper cookware, stores plates.

LEFT:

The L-shaped working area in this Colonial-style kitchen is screened, on the dining-room side, by a primitive step-back cupboard, which also makes room for an eat-in table near to the cooking area. Chopping-block counters provide an excellent work surface, and the tile back splash is both easy to maintain and adds a handsome decorative element that coordinates with the cabinets. A rag rug in the sink area softens the brick floor, and the chandelier over the hutch breakfast table combines candles with an electric bulb hidden within a punctured tin shade.

In this open, airy, and well-organized kitchen, simple wooden shelves on iron brackets display working collectibles on a wall area too small to accommodate cabinets. The counter in the foreground is cleverly cantilevered over a base cabinet to permit room for eating outside the work area. Wood-grained paneling disguises the dishwasher to the right of the sink. Wooden floors in a traditional kitchen can be easily maintained, provided they are adequately protected by at least four coats of polyurethane varnish and waxed occasionally.

In this open, airy, and well-organized kitchen, simple wooden shelves on iron brackets display working collectibles on a wall area too small to accommodate cabinets. The counter in the foreground is cleverly cantilevered over a base cabinet to permit room for eating outside the work area. Wood-grained paneling disguises the dishwasher to the right of the sink. Wooden floors in a traditional kitchen can be easily maintained, provided they are adequately protected by at least four coats of polyurethane varnish and waxed from time to time.

OPPOSITE PAGE:

In modernizing this turn-of-the-century-style kitchen, old wall cabinets with glass doors were retained but new base cabinets were installed under the window area. A generously sized island was added for extra work and storage space plus an additional sink. The marble-topped counters are a pastry cook's dream come true.

as almost any color you might want. Or you may prefer to use ceramic or quarry tile, butcher block, or stainless steel. For cutting purposes and pastry making, a natural, unfinished butcher block surface is highly recommended.

Kitchen Storage

Base and wall-hung cabinets are most commonly used for kitchen storage. They may be custom-made to your exact requirements, or you can choose from a variety of factory-made cabinets in styles that range from simply utilitarian to paneled French provincial. The number of cabinets you will need depends on how much you want to store and the amount of available space in your kitchen. In a larger room you may decide on base cabinets only and use the wall space to hang attractive pots and pans, molds, colanders, and other interesting cookware. Wall shelves can be used for a display of collectibles, as well as for dishes and comestibles.

Base cabinets. A typical factory-made base cabinet is 36 inches high and 24 inches deep. It has a counter top, a drawer or two, and two shelves at the bottom, which may be stationary or adjustable and are covered by doors. Stationary shelves can waste storage space and create a jumble of oddly sized items that can be difficult to sort out. Since base cabinets are available in widths that are multiples of three inches, with a minimum width of nine inches, it is possible to order sizes to suit your individual needs in terms of space as well as storage. Look for base cabinets with properly sized drawers; pull-out shelves for storing pots and pans, lids, cooking utensils, and flatware; vertical dividers for trays and cookie sheets, as well as adjustable shelves for storing anything from canned goods to small appliances. If a base cabinet turns a corner, install a cabinet equipped with a lazy susan that revolves, making anything on it easily accessible, and make sure the lazy susan is as deep as possible to take full advantage of the space.

Allowing adequate space for appliances. Because frontage sizes vary with different models and manufacturers, it is best to select the appliances before planning the cabinets. But if the kitchen must be planned before deciding on the appliances, allow 36 inches for a refrigerator and for a double-bowl sink (24 inches for a single-bowl sink), 30 inches for a range or built-in surface unit, and 24 inches each for a built-in oven or dishwasher. A wall or ceiling fan or a hood with a built-in vent should be installed above the range. If you decide on a hood, it should be installed to allow a clear view of the back burners; if the depth of the hood, from front to back, is 17 inches or less, the bottom of the hood should be 56 inches from the floor; if it is 18 inches or more, the distance above the floor should be 60 inches.

*Because the oven is the least used of all the major kitchen
appliances, the location of separate built-in ovens does not have to
be within the work triangle—the busy area between the stove, sink,
and refrigerator. In this U-shaped arrangement, a work island
adds room for a sink and for eating, plus counter space, and extra
storage. Pine paneling unites the upper walls and cabinets and
complements the look of brick.*

OPPOSITE PAGE:

*An old step-back cupboard against a kitchen wall makes a
handsome repository for a display of late–nineteenth- and early–
twentieth-century blue-and-white ceramic pitchers and labeled
canisters. The slatted blue crate on the floor once carried eggs to
market; the three-legged stool was used for milking cows.*

BELOW:

An old pie cupboard, its tin doors punctured in a pleasing pattern for ventilation, holds an eclectic collection of enamelware pots and ceramic bowls, plus apple-faced dolls representing a farmer and his wife.

Wall-hung cabinets. A typical wall-hung cabinet is 30 inches high and 12 inches deep. Like base cabinets, wall cabinets are made in multiples of three-inch widths but in a minimum width of 12 inches. Wall cabinets should be placed about 15 inches above the counter to allow clearance for small appliances, and the top shelf should be within six feet of the floor for easy reaching. The amount of china, glassware, serving dishes, and groceries to be stored will more or less determine how many wall cabinets you will need. Three adjustable shelves within each cabinet allow leeway for storing various sizes of glassware or serving pieces as well as food. Ideally, wall cabinets should be located near the sink or dining area and above counter work centers; if placed above a sink, refrigerator, or built-in oven, they are not easily accessible, but they provide storage for seldom-used articles.

196

Ambiance

Unless it's exceptionally small, a purely functional area can be turned into a friendly and inviting room. Even an existing kitchen can be made to serve more than one purpose by the judicious choice and arrangement of movable or built-in furniture. A desk tucked into one corner, an attractive bookcase to display your best serving pieces or cookbooks, a shelf for kitchen collectibles, all add interest. But whatever size your kitchen may be, do make room for at least a snack bar with stools, if not for a table and chairs. If you *have* the room, you might even consider placing a small sofa or comfortable chair in the kitchen! This is an excellent way to visit with friends or family while preparing food.

ABOVE:

In this kitchen/dining room, cabinets serving the L-shaped working area create a bright background for leisurely dining near the corner fireplace. A wine storage rack replaces one base cabinet; open shelves above it store colorful dinnerware.

Bathrooms

Bathrooms were a novelty during the late nineteenth century when indoor plumbing was first installed in what had been previously a bedroom in most homes. A working bathroom usually contained a generous-size tub, a pedestal sink, and a pull-chain toilet with a water tank on the wall. Today, there is a wide choice of basic equipment in white or a multitude of colors and a number of sizes and styles, plus all sorts of extras, such as whirlpool tubs, bidets, pulsating shower heads that also conserve hot water, water-saving toilets, and even heated towel racks.

The plan of a bathroom depends on how it will be used. If the room is to be shared by two or more people and space allows, it is most convenient if the room is divided into separate areas for the toilet, tub and/or shower, and a double lavatory to be shared during the morning rush hour. If you are building or remodeling, think about whether or not you might want to include a sauna, a hot tub, an exercise center, or even some form of greenhouse to fill with plants.

For either new construction or a major renovation, it is always best to discuss your ideas with an architect. The simple replacement of fixtures with newer, more efficient models can be handled by a plumber alone; relocating fixtures or adding extra ones may cause problems that should be solved by a contractor.

An old door with a boldly stenciled label is the first clue to whimsey in this dare-to-be different powder room. The old washing machine, complete with clothes wringer, is equipped with an old-style sink. Above it, a salvaged medicine cabinet is painted bright red to match the panel on the door; coat hangers hold red and blue towels. The humorous clock and old washboard on the wall are appropriate finishing touches.

Storage in a bathroom is often a problem. Here it is solved by converting an old kitchen cabinet into a combination lavatory medicine chest and storage closet for bathroom linen. Cheerful red-and-white wallpaper applied to the panels of the cabinet make it blend into the walls, reducing its apparent bulk. Recyclable pieces of this type can often be found at tag sales, in junk yards or, refinished, in antiques shops.

If you plan to replace a lavatory, you might want to add under-the-sink storage by choosing a ready-made vanity or by enclosing the sink with custom-made cabinetry that has shelves designed for special needs. Decorative shelves on the wall above the toilet are ideal for holding attractive jars of soap, bathpowder, small linens, or other purely decorative accessories.

Your wardrobe of towels and bathmats can be as boldly patterned, colorful, and varied as you like, offering a different look with each change of linen. And, if there is sufficient daylight, include at least one growing plant for a living touch; it will thrive in the humid atmosphere.

Because moisture is common in a bathroom, walls, floor, and ceiling should be impervious to its problems. If you use paint, semi-gloss or gloss is easier to clean and simple to apply. Use gloss on the woodwork. If you are adding new wall surfaces, you can choose from among various moisture-resistant types—ceramic tile, wood planks, plastic-laminated panels, vinyl or vinyl-coated wall coverings. If a vinyl wall covering is chosen, you can preserve it longer by leaving the bathroom door slightly ajar whenever the room is steamy. Floors may be wood planks, ceramic or resilient tile, or cushioned sheet goods.

A mirror with strong light on both sides is a necessity for applying makeup and for shaving; general illumination can be supplied by built-in spotlights, wall sconces, or fluorescent fixtures. If the room is small, a mirrored wall will make it seem larger and will add reflected light.

CHAPTER THIRTEEN

Accessories and collectibles

After all the essential elements of room decoration have been established—furniture, color scheme, floor and wall coverings, lighting, window treatment—accessories and collectibles are the distinctive finishing touches that add ambiance and interest to every room, stamping it with your very own unique personality.

Basically, there are two kinds of accessories. Some are both decorative and functional. Clocks, mirrors, pillows, waste-baskets, and linens for bed and bath fall into this category. Others, such as pictures, plants, or flower arrangements, simply please the eye while adding charm to the room. Collect-ibles can fall within either category. If your style is country-minded, for example, a primitive bench could function as a coffee table or a collection of Currier & Ives prints could decorate a wall. The important thing is to accessorize your home in a way that pleases you and with things that appeal to your own sense of what is right and beautiful.

How to Choose Accessories and Collectibles

Overall, there are no rigid rules to follow in choosing accessories, but there are a few basic guidelines. Whether selecting for functional use or visual pleasure, always pick things that reflect your own taste and life-style. Accessories can supply a bright accent in a neutral color scheme or, in a room full of several colors, they can provide a unifying element when repeated in

OPPOSITE PAGE:

Accessories and collectibles bring this Colonial bedroom alive by picking up the subtle touch of red in the stencil pattern that rings the top of the walls. The same bright red is repeated in the pillow on the wing chair in the coverings on both beds—adult and doll size (under the table)—and in the framed children's drawings on the wall above the child's chair.

A hooked rug with a charmingly primitive farm scene, a carefully worked child's sampler, a folk art bird perched on a simple box, a graduated stack of small boxes, a rag doll sitting on a child's chair—all share the same naively appealing character as the wallpaper.

OPPOSITE PAGE:

A double-tiered bureau at the foot of a bed provides a perfect stage for an array of children's treasures. On the top tier, pull toys parade in orderly fashion before a colorful background of youngster's books; on the second tier a well-used teddy bear and two cloth dolls keep company with a worn calico cat and some more pull toys.

several places. Keep your color scheme in mind when considering larger pieces such as big pillows or a folding screen. Don't hesitate to combine old things with new, but do make sure that most of your functional accessories share the same mood— formal or informal, simple or sophisticated. You can be as daring as you like with your purely decorative pieces: Primitive folk art, for example, can add simple charm to a sophisticated formal room.

You need not spend a fortune on your accessories and collectibles. You can pick up appealing and interesting things, old or new, at tag sales, thrift shops, or flea markets. Excellent reproductions of paintings and sculpture can be found in museum gift shops, most of which offer catalogs for ordering by mail. Collections of almost anything—from seashells or interesting pebbles gathered on trips to the beach to gnarled and weathered pieces of wood found in the forest—can add interest and character when successfully displayed.

Create Your Own Treasures

When you travel, take snapshots of anything that you find particularly appealing and interesting—buildings, road signs, landscapes, people. Your best shots, grouped within one large frame or blown up and framed individually, will be a daily reminder of your happy trip. Or try your hand at needlepoint for uniquely beautiful wall hangings, pillows, or seat covers, all stitched in your very own colors. You can also use easy-to-follow stamped or transfer patterns to decorate curtains, linens, pillows, or towels. Or work with ceramics, watercolors, oil paints, or decoupage to create your own personal treasures.

If you have any talent for painting, decorated tinware known as tole is another type of traditional accessory you can make yourself. Hobby shops can supply the basic tin forms—trays, boxes, canisters, and tea and coffee pots are a few of the many possibilities. Black, red, and green are the most traditional background colors for tole work, but you need not be limited in your choice. Depending on your talent, you can add colorful designs—anything from a simple floral or stylized leaf pattern to a detailed portrait of your house. If your painting style is primitive, so much the better; you will have created your own folk art.

Try new uses for things you already own but seldom use. Search your cupboards for handsome jars and pitchers that could be used to hold an arrangement of flowers or leaves, interesting coffee mugs to store pens and pencils on a desk, attractive casseroles to serve as planters, a generous basket to store your magazines and newspapers. These are just a few of the almost endless possibilities.

Displaying Your Treasures

Purely decorative accessories and collectibles can be arranged on walls, tabletops, shelves, sideboards, chests—any surface

For greater visual impact, collections of smaller things should be grouped together. Here a family of teddy bears faces a family of rag dolls; all are snugly and comfortably ensconced on a child's wagon seat.

Wall arrangements need not be limited to framed pictures—anything collectible and hangable can contribute character and interest to an interior. The view from this stairwell, dominated by a merry-go-round horse, includes a collection of enameled-tin store signs on the upstairs hallway wall and a carefully hung grouping of small spice chests in the downstairs foyer.

that offers space not in active use is a likely candidate for an effective display.

In planning your arrangements, you should also think in terms of focal points, either natural or created. If you are blessed with a fireplace as your natural focal point, its functional andirons and fire tools can also be considered as decorative accessories and should be chosen to complement your overall scheme. For an early American mood use primitive wrought-iron or simple brass tools and andirons; on the mantlepiece you might want to consider a mixture of pewter plates and tankards with wrought-iron candlesticks. For a more formal, late colonial look, use more ornately designed brass or steel fireplace equipment; on the mantle you could have a traditionally styled clock, balanced by a collection of porcelain pieces or finely wrought brass candlesticks. If you don't have a fireplace, you can create a focal point by grouping several pictures on one wall or one large picture over your sofa.

Wall Arrangements

Proportion is all-important in wall arrangements. Consider the size and shape of the piece of furniture beneath any wall arrangement—a single large picture should not exceed the width of a sofa, buffet, chest, or other objects beneath it, nor should an arrangement of several pictures exceed some visual limit.

Wall arrangements need not be limited to framed pictures, and pictures need not be limited to original works of art; reproductions of oil paintings, watercolors, engravings—all by great artists—are available in great variety and at small cost. Or you may want to invest in a limited-edition original print pulled from a metal plate, stone slab, or woodblock prepared by the artist. They are reasonably priced, and when signed and numbered, they often increase in value.

Rather than limiting wall arrangements to pictures, you might want to include sconces, a cordless clock, a piece of sculpture, a collection of porcelain, or three-dimensional folk art—whatever strikes your fancy and seems appropriate.

Most people are completely intimidated by the thought of grouping a number of pictures and/or objects on a wall, fearing that they will end up with a lopsided arrangement plus possible damage to the wall itself. Instead of pounding a handful of picture hooks into the wall in a haphazard fashion, hoping for a balanced result, try out your ideas for an arrangement on the floor before pounding a single nail. Spread the elements on a piece of brown paper the size of the wall area to be covered. Try each element of the arrangement in a variety of possible positions until you hit upon a balanced effect that pleases you. Then trace the outline of each piece and mark the points where picture hooks will meet the wire on the back. Punch a small hole through the paper for each picture hook and by

Picture Arrangements

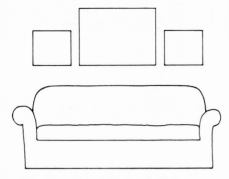

Align the bottom edges of several pictures in a symmetrical arrangement that matches the length of the furniture beneath them.

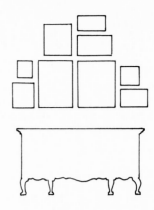

Build an interesting pyramid shape that will add height to the room, and balance the furniture beneath it.

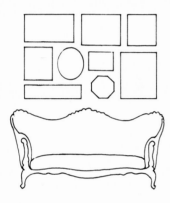

Arrange a group of pictures of various shapes so that their outside edges form a perfect square.

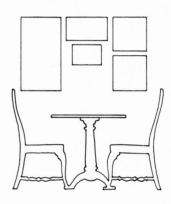

Align several pictures at the sides and top only, so that the furniture beneath them balances the grouping.

Create a well-balanced circular arrangement of various sizes as an attractive focal point.

Balance an asymmetric grouping with a strong vertical, such as a large plant.

code, or some other method, identify each element on the paper plan. Tape the paper to the wall, pencil the hook position on the wall through each hole, remove the paper, and then pound the picture hooks into the wall.

If you are hanging only one picture, have someone hold it against the wall for you, and move it about until you find the perfect location. Then mark the spot on the wall where the picture wire will meet the hook, and then anchor the hook.

Standard nail and metal picture hangers come in different sizes to support weights from light to heavy. Mirrors, for example, weigh more than a framed watercolor, and so be sure to use the right size hook for the weight of the object. And avoid possible damage to plaster walls by applying a small cross of self-adhesive tape to the wall before pounding in the nail. For lightweight objects, you may prefer to use cloth-supported hooks; simply wet the gummed cloth, press it firmly against the wall, and hang the object after the cloth has dried completely.

For difficult surfaces such as glass, tile, brick, or stone, double-adhesive strips are available that come with a protective paper backing on both sides. Simply remove the paper backing from one side and press it against the object to be hung; then remove the remaining paper and press the object firmly against the wall in the *exact* position desired—once attached it can only be removed by cutting through the foam adhesive.

If you collect anything hangable—trivets, tiles, early tools, quilts—share your treasures by displaying them on the wall.

Handsome old quilts are very much a part of our design heritage, and their display need not be limited to covering beds; whether antique or newly made, their fascinating pattern, texture, and combination of colors can enrich the walls of any room. Above the quilt in the foreground is hung a collection of old metal quilting patterns.

Displaying Quilts

Handsome quilts, with their fascinating pattern, texture, and colors, are very much a part of our design heritage. Antique quilts made as recently as the late nineteenth or early twentieth century have skyrocketed in price, but it is still possible to find bargains in out-of-the-way country auctions or antique shops. You can also find machine-made reproductions that cost considerably less than handmade antiques.

If you love quilts, as most of us do, you need not limit their use to gracing your beds. Whether your quilt is twin-, full-, or crib-size, it will add charm and interest to a living room, family room, or bedroom wall—even a foyer. And there are safe ways to hang it without damaging the sometimes delicate material.

Of course, the quilt can be framed by a professional, but the cost is usually considerable, however simple the frame. The easiest method consists of stitching a muslin casing on the back of the quilt all the way across the top, making it deep enough to accommodate a simple curtain rod with an invisible mounting or a café rod with decorative brackets. Then slip the rod through the casing and hang the quilt. Be sure to use a rod sturdy enough to support the weight of the quilt, which is sometimes considerable.

Displaying Smaller Items

Collections of smaller things should be displayed together for maximum interest and impact. Whether you have three paperweights or thirty, group them together on a tabletop, a shelf, or in a miniature cupboard hanging on the wall.

If your dining room has a corner cupboard, hutch, or other open cabinet, use it to display your best china, glassware, and serving pieces—anything beautiful that is related to dining. If you have a collection of unusual plates you might want to show them on a plate rail high on the dining-room wall, out of danger of being broken. A dining table needs only an attractive centerpiece of some sort—an arrangement of flowers, a bowl of fruit, or a plant in a decorative cache pot.

Kitchen Displays

A kitchen can also be livened by a display of handsome cookware and collectibles related to cooking, such as old breadboards, graters, or canisters. Whatever your interest might be will also be interesting to others. Pots and pans of copper, enamelware, iron, stainless steel, or copper; ceramic molds; clear glass jars filled with pasta and other dried foods; or baskets or bowls filled with vegetables or fruit—all add color and interest to what might otherwise be an ordinary kitchen.

If your kitchen is large enough to have wall space to spare, some that is not taken up by cabinets, you might want to hang a collection of old or new cookie cutters, cutting boards, rolling pins, colanders—anything collectible that is related to cooking. You will always need the basic functional accessories, whatever size your kitchen might be. You can always find room for your cookbooks, even if you have to add a shelf to hold them or store them at the back of a counter, held in place by a pair of canisters rather than the usual bookends. And to please both your eye and your palate, include a living touch with as many pots of herbs—anything from chives to rosemary—as you can accommodate.

Bathroom Displays

The bath is the one room that depends almost entirely on accessories for glamor and comfort; strangely, it is also the room most usually neglected in accessorizing a house. There's no need for that; the array of coordinated colors and patterns in bath towels, shower curtains, and rugs can make the plainest bathroom look exciting. In addition, try putting an interesting frame around a stock mirror; use "unbathroomy" lighting fixtures—a chandelier, electrified gas lamps, wall sconces; investigate the many different designs in faucet fixtures. There is never enough storage space in a bathroom; install open shelves

Vulnerable treasures are most dramatically and safely displayed within a lighted cabinet. Here a collection of early majolica earthenware is further enhanced by a tracery of bittersweet cuttings.

OPPOSITE PAGE:

Until the advent of plastic and cardboard, shelves in shops were lined with lithographed tin containers used to package everything from tea to tobacco. The youngest container in this collection is the Camel tin on the second shelf from the top; during the 1950s, popular brands were packaged in this way to hold fifty cigarettes.

Blue-and-white enamel cookware, supplemented by an earthenware pitcher and bowl, fill and top a primitive corner cupboard—even spill over onto nearby walls. Any kitchen with wall space to spare can be enlivened by a display of collectibles related to cooking.

Drawers that once held printer's type are an effective means of displaying anything small enough to fit within their many partitions. Don't be afraid to mix old with new or feel obliged to stick within one category—the more varied the assortment of miniatures, the better.

RIGHT:

A collection of intricately shaped and decorated green and white majolica fills the shelves of this elegant French provincial dresser, creating a focal point of color in the room's neutral color scheme.

BELOW:

A dining-room cupboard is an ideal place to store and display treasured dinnerware safely. This collection of antique china and pressed glass is arranged for balance and convenience, with the least used pieces on the top shelf.

and brackets to hold attractively packaged toiletries, pretty containers for soaps and other necessities, stacks of colorful towels. Extra towel bars and rings, a hamper, a small bench or stool, a transistor clock, and a bathroom scale are great conveniences, and a wall telephone is pure luxury. Plants such as fern, ivy, or philodendron thrive in the moist atmosphere of a bathroom, if they are placed near a window for light.

Flowers as Accessories

Every room needs the added touch of purely decorative accessories that add life and color, and it's easy to do in a number of different ways. During the growing season you can fill your house with exuberant arrangements of garden flowers; during the winter months you can substitute dried arrangements of flowers, grasses, or autumn leaves—even delicately shaped bare branches, either in their natural color or spray painted for further definition.

Houseplants can be a cheerful year-round living addition to any room with a window; lacking a window, they will still thrive if placed beneath special lights that promote growth. A florist or nursery can supply potted plants for sunny or shady windows, and information on which plants require green-thumb pampering and those that will tolerate indifference. You can choose plants for their interesting foliage, such as a number of different ferns, ivys, and philodendron, or plants, like the amaryllis, that bloom either in a spectacular burst that lasts two or three weeks, or those that go on patiently producing blossoms over a period of months. You can fill a tray with a fascinating collection of miniature cacti, or you can train a vine to frame a window filled with houseplants on glass shelves.

Small trees that can live happily indoors, like the jade or Norfolk pine, are also great attention-getters. Just as architects sometimes correct their visual mistakes with landscaping, masking a dull and windowless wall with a vigorous planting of shrubbery, you can fill a corner in a sparsely furnished room with a large potted tree and help it to thrive with a grow bulb set behind a spotlight to add a nighttime pattern of fascinating shadows.

No matter what touch you or your family give it, every room should in some way reflect the presence or personality of those who live in it. It is these very individual accents that will make any house a home.

A collection of old hotel napkins recycled into pillow covers adds strong color and striking pattern to an otherwise plain sofa. With a little imagination and ingenuity unexpected and clever uses can often be found for collectibles you may already own.

OPPOSITE PAGE:

The diversity of size and shape in this collection of duck and shore bird decoys makes it more appealing and interesting, and the careful placement of each bird to create balance and symmetry on all six shelves makes a harmonious composition.

CHAPTER FOURTEEN

From old
to new

Nothing is quite so satisfying as falling in love with a charming old building, buying it for a song, and rescuing it from oblivion by converting it into a comfortable home. Here is a varied assortment of five unlike structures, each remodeled with imagination, careful planning, and tender care.

From One-Room Schoolhouse to Country Retreat

With a little bit of luck it is still possible to find a small abandoned schoolhouse that can be easily converted into a charming cottage. This classic example was sturdily built of stone, outlasting the generations of children who studied here to finally become a compact and comfortable home.

Structural changes involved new windows, doors, and the addition of a weathertight roof. Except for partitioning a corner area to create space for a bathroom, an open plan prevails throughout the house, with living, dining, and kitchen areas flowing effortlessly from one into the next.

A bedroom was gained by adding a sleeping loft over the bathroom and kitchen area. The weathered barn-siding paneling is in keeping with the rural character of the house, and an allover pattern on red-background wallpaper, used on an end wall, emphasizes the high sloping ceiling.

OPPOSITE PAGE:

An unusually high ceiling offered the needed space for creating a sleeping loft overlooking the living room. An extra-long old pine bench, beautifully refinished, serves as a coffee table for the comfortable wing chair and contemporary sofa.

217

The old stone building has a commanding view of orchards and rolling farmland. The exterior required only fresh paint for the trim and a new front door.

In this living room, subtle contrasts in pattern and texture are provided architecturally by vertically paneled walls, the horizontal lines of the brick wall, and the plank floor, as well as by the decorative details of the braided rug and the linear patterns in the fabrics.

ABOVE:

The compact kitchen is semiscreened from the living room by a breakfast bar fitted with old ice-cream parlor stools. An antique regulator clock is a reminder of schoolhouse days.

LEFT:

In the dining area, wainscoting of weathered barnsiding was added, which is newly papered with a traditional all-over pattern. Tableware is stored in the primitive corner cupboard and country-type paneled chest.

A spiral staircase leads directly to a new deck, added to create additional space for living, dining, and entertaining.

From Storage Space to Living Space

Originally used only for storage, the upper floor of this suburban garage was successfully converted into an attractive and comfortable three-room apartment. Architectural additions to the structurally sound old building included new windows and skylights for much needed light and ventilation, plus a deck that added space for outdoor living, dining, and entertaining. A new spiral staircase provided direct access to the deck; there is another "bad weather" entrance through the garage and up a stairway.

Interior space was thoughtfully planned to make the best possible use of a comparatively small area. The end result is a charmingly formal living room, a compact kitchen and bath, and a handsome bedroom that also serves as a den.

ABOVE:

Bookshelves that turn a corner in the living room add visual height as well as a display area for collectibles. A handsome area rug defines the conversation grouping.

LEFT:

A new skylight in the compact kitchen provides ventilation and sunlight for a thriving plant. Positive and negative versions of the same pattern are played against each other in curtains, walls, and ceiling.

The same delicate pattern covering walls, ceiling, and window is repeated in a darker color on the armchair and antique iron bed to coordinate the whole room. An old trunk, serving as a table, adds storage.

New Life for an Old Home

Like so many early nineteenth-century houses in the Midwest, the left side of this shingled house began life in 1826 as a log cabin; the "new" wing on the right was added in 1836, and it was probably at that time that shingles, conforming to the later building, were added to the original structure.

The house was basically sound and required only minor repairs plus cosmetic .work, such as staining the shingles and painting the trim. In the original wing, layers of crumbling plaster were removed to reveal sturdy handhewn logs, and in the kitchen and dining room, old pine floor boards were stripped of layers of paint to display their natural grain and were then sealed with polyurethane to protect their beauty. Industrial carpeting, with the look and texture of early carpet, was chosen to cover the living-room floor.

LEFT:

In 1836 a wing was added at right angles to the original 1826 log cabin house on the left. Doorways, windows, and shutters have remained unchanged through the years.

OPPOSITE PAGE:

Except for upholstered pieces, antique furnishings and collectibles prevail throughout the house. A bullet-punctured weather vane decorates the stripped pine mantel; a collection of decoys is highlighted at the window.

Quarry tile, softened by a rag rug, now paves the entrance hall. Original panels in the handsome old door were outlined with white paint; antique leaded glass replaced the old frosted panels.

OPPOSITE PAGE:
Layers of crumbling plaster in the old wing were removed to reveal hand-hewn logs once chinked with wood chips and now dramatized by new plaster. Handmade rag rugs add a colorful accent over the industrial carpeting on the living-room floor.

The updated eighteenth-century schoolhouse presents a classic limestone facade graced by a newly added stoop and doorway. To bring more light and a feeling of outdoor space to the back of the house, a sunken terrace was created by excavating the area and paving it with flagstone. An indoor view of the terrace and garden was made possible by installing a large window in the cellar living room.

From an Eighteenth-Century Schoolhouse to a Twentieth-Century Home

After generations of neglect, this sizable limestone building in an upstate New York village has been restored to dignity. A major portion of the restoration involved removing a wooden late-nineteenth-century addition from the left side of the house to again reveal the complete classic shape of the original building. A new front stoop and doorway replaced the old side entrance.

Generations of debris were removed from the basement to uncover an eighteenth-century hearth with sturdy masonry walls. The fireplace was put in working order, a cement floor was poured and painted, a large window was installed, and the once dismal basement became a charming living room looking out on the garden. Outdoor living space was added by excavating an area beyond the cellar-door entrance and paving it with flagstone.

It took thirteen years of diligent work and loving attention to detail to complete this noble restoration; the old schoolhouse is now a perfect background for the owner's antique furniture and an eclectic assortment of collectibles.

After removing generations of debris from the cellar, the original eighteenth-century hearth and masonry walls were uncovered. The doorway at the left leads to the terrace shown on the opposite page below.

A handwoven bird-of-paradise coverlet graces a finely carved cannonball bed; quilts are stored in the old chest at its foot. The pine chest-of-drawers/secretary and an antique washstand add further storage in the room.

OPPOSITE PAGE ABOVE:

In the formal parlor on the main floor, the original molding has been carefully restored to create a pleasing pattern against the white walls. A daybed/sofa and Victorian armchair are grouped for easy conversation.

BELOW:

In the cellar, an informal living room with its new window looks out on the garden. Old log beams were retained; the dirt floor was paved with cement and painted barn red.

A Deserted Cottage Becomes a Gracious Home

This early nineteenth-century building was physically sound, but the interior required complete renovation—new plaster walls; the refinishing of the floors, woodwork, and beams; the installation of a kitchen and bathroom; and the replacement of a wooden stairway with a space-saving spiral iron staircase.

Careful planning enabled the new owner to get a maximum amount of livable space within a comparatively small building. Most of the main floor is devoted to a gracious and formal living room with a small dining alcove and a compact kitchen; upstairs, into a bedroom/study and a bathroom.

Throughout the small house, comfortable contemporary pieces are mixed with fine antique furniture and collectibles. In every room, flower arrangements and growing plants add a living touch.

OPPOSITE PAGE:

A new flagstone terrace is a pleasant expansion of living and dining space during the summer months.

BELOW:

Custom cabinets in the compact kitchen are furnished with strap hinges and porcelain knobs. Built-in fluorescent fixtures high-light counter work areas.

The living room combines contemporary comfort with mellow antiques. A newly installed spiral staircase leads to the up-stairs bedroom/study.

A bed/sofa is tucked cozily into the dormer area of the upstairs bedroom study. Built-in ceiling spotlights provide general illumination; a three-candle lamp lights the handsome desk.

Ladderback chairs in the dining alcove are supplemented by a primitive country bench. Since privacy isn't a factor to consider, the casement windows here and throughout the house are left uncurtained to let in as much light as possible.

At one end of the living room, the handsome pattern and texture of the old stone wall create a dramatic background for the tall case clock.

Appendix

WORKING WITH
PROFESSIONALS

Architects and interior designers can contribute invaluably to the success of any major project. If you have any doubts concerning your own taste and judgment, it would be wise to get professional help. Even if you are fairly sure of what you want, you can often save considerable time and money by seeking the help of an expert.

Whether you are building a house or doing extensive remodeling, the services of a qualified architect can eliminate the necessity of living with expensive mistakes in planning. Trained as they are to think in terms of converting space into maximum livability, architects can offer fresh, workable ideas that can mean the difference between a result that is barely acceptable and one that is eminently attractive and comfortable.

Because even the most talented architect is not a mind reader, he or she will need input from you. Provide a thorough rundown on your life-style, and explain what features you would like to incorporate and the look you hope to achieve. If you have kept a file of pictures that you hope to make into a reality for yourself, turn it over to him or her with a list of top priorities; your budget may eliminate some of your hopes, but you might also be able to retain the most important ones.

How to Find an Architect

Builders, contractors, and banks can provide you with the names of architects working in your area. Or perhaps a friend or an acquaintance has had a successful experience in working with an architect. As a last resort, you can check the Yellow Pages of the telephone directory. Any architect with the initials *A.I.A.* after the name has been examined and found qualified by the American Institute of Architects. The A.I.A. has also established a code of ethics that all members must abide by. When you see an architect, ask for examples of his or her work to see if you like the results and the names of clients with whom you can check.

For additional help in establishing a satisfactory contract with an architect, write to the Publications Office of the American Institute of Architects, 457 Madison Avenue, New York, N.Y. 10022. They have a number of different model contracts suitable for various needs.

In general, it is important to make sure that you receive from any architect or contractor a full written estimate of any work to be done. This should include a detailed breakdown of the specific materials, appliances, hardware, and other objects to be installed; the time it will take to complete the job (you might want to include a penalty clause for lateness or a bonus for early completion); a guarantee of insurance coverage for any laborers that will be on the premises; and, of course, a detailed breakdown of each part of the total cost and a payment schedule. It is best to divide the payment into an advance—usually a third, another third when the job is two-thirds completed, the final third on satisfactory completion of work.

What about Fees?

You will need to have a frank discussion with any architect or contractor you choose about the amount you can afford to pay for the entire project. The fee will depend on how deeply you expect him or her to become involved with the job.

Full architectural service includes designing and supplying working blueprints and a list of specified materials needed, selecting a reliable contractor, and overseeing the work through every step. A complete service of this type usually amounts to 15 percent of the construction costs. An architect's charge can also be a flat fee for designing and supplying working blueprints, leaving it up to you to carry through with a contractor. Or if you feel that you only need to clarify your own ideas, consultation fees usually range widely and may be figured on an hourly or daily rate, depending on how much help you need.

In working with an architect, always be open and honest about what you really want. If some of the suggestions are not to your liking, tell him or her that you would prefer another solution to that particular problem. Since you will be living with the work, the architect's first mission is to satisfy your needs.

Working with a Designer

Many of the same principles apply whether you are working with an architect or an interior designer. Again, you must make your wants, needs, and your taste preferences known. Like architects, interior designers will work with you for a consultation fee or will take on the entire job, usually for a percentage of the cost of furnishings purchased for your home.

When doing an entire job, a designer will shop for everything needed, present a scheme in sketch form that includes color samples, fabric swatches, and a rendering of how the room will look with everything in place. One advantage in hiring a designer is gaining access to showrooms that offer unusual furnishings not usually available in retail stores.

How to Find a Designer

The American Society of Interior Designers has established stringent examinations and a code of ethics for would-be members; those who qualify are allowed to use the initials *A.S.I.D.* after their names. Most towns of any size have resident designers listed in the Yellow Pages.

Some of the larger furniture and department stores offer the services of an in-house designer who will guide you in choosing from the merchandise available in that particular store. Service of this type usually, but not always, involves contracting to buy a certain amount of merchandise from the store, and the choice is usually limited to what the store carries.

Whether you opt for an independent designer or one who works for a store, it is important to feel comfortable with that person. Ideally there should be mutual respect between you— the designer should bend to your particular taste and needs, and you should respect the designer's taste and judgment. Once that is established, also be sure that you receive a signed copy of any orders that you may have agreed to, along with a sample of any pertinent swatches to avoid possible misunderstandings.

CREDITS

PHOTOGRAPHERS

Photographs in Chapter 1, courtesy of The Art Institute of Chicago; all other photographs courtesy of *Good Housekeeping* and *Country Living* magazines.

Jerry Abramowitz: 182, 209.
Ernst Beadle: 64, 71, 88, 103, 138, 207
Herb Bleiweiss: 211
Cooper & Coughlin: 42, 127
Edgar De Evia: 180
Feliciano: 84, 86, 128
Howard Graff: 49
Stephen Green-Armytage: 208, 212-213
Joshua Greene: 53
Richard Jeffrey: 178-179, 188-189, 212, 222-225
Paul Kopelow: 50, 134
Elyse Lewin: 59
Vince Lisanti: 44, 58, 60, 64
Chris Mead: 138-139, 161, 189
Keith Scott Morton: 32, 35, 39, 40, 41, 55, 62, 70, 74, 78-79, 83, 91, 93, 100, 104, 109, 110, 113, 129, 145, 148, 149, 172, 182, 187, 190-191, 200, 202, 204, 214, 215
Charles Nesbit: 116, 230, 233
Frances Pellegrini: 36-37
Philip Roedel: 66-67, 170, 234-240
Will Rousseau: 10
Dick Sharpe: 86, 89, 195, 216, 218-221, 226-229
William P. Steele: 114
Jessie Walker: 34, 45, 65, 68, 72, 90, 98, 116, 117, 118, 121, 141, 152, 162, 165, 166, 167, 171, 192, 193, 194, 196, 197, 198, 199, 203, 205, 210, 216, 218-221, 226-229
Susan Wood: 184
Don Zimmerman: 124-125

DESIGNERS AND ARCHITECTS

Patricia Adams: 171, 216, 218-219, 220, 221
C.F. Brasch and Raphael Sullivan: 50
Sue and Neil Connell: 41, 78-79
Jane Cottingham: 35, 129, 190-191
Country Interiors: 42, 127

Sven E. Danielson: 66-67, 234, 235, 236-237, 238, 239, 240
Abby Darer: 128
John Drummond: 152
Barbara Ellsley: 100
Jan Farley: 72
Charles L. Flint: 70
Edith G. Gillman: 22, 223, 224-225
Diane Gove: 116
Phyllis Haders: 64, 103, 138, 196-197
Mark Hampton: 90, 117
Celia Hubbard: 36-37
Stan Hura and Chuck Giordano: 109
Dean Ingram: 84
Kevin Mayo and Ralph De Lucci: 145, 149
Robert Metzger: 74
Pam Myers: 45, 98, 162, 192
Richard Lowell Neas: 189
Rachel Newman: 93
Louis Nichole: 182
Bo Niles: 139
Sylvia Parker: 59
Marilyn Radloff: 34, 226, 227, 228, 229
Alfred E. Scheffer: 184
Herbert and Margaret Schiffer: 58
Kathy Schoemer: 39, 200, 202, 204
Allen Scruggs and Douglas Myers: 44, 60, 62, 64, 83, 104, 110, 113, 148-149, 182
Steve Smallman: 55
Earl Vaughn: 121, 167
Adelaide Vincent: 116, 230, 231, 232, 233
Raymond Waites: 91
Diana White: 53, 170, 40
Nina Williams: 32

OTHER

Stenciling: Kenneth Fortnay, 10
    Adele Bishop, 71, 88
Rosemaling: Betty Wagner, 68
Ironwork: Stanley Gove, 166
Furniture design: Peter Kramer, 118
Wallpainting: Virginia Teichner, 100
Information provided for portions of Chapters 5, 6, 8, and 12, courtesy Cooperative Extension Services of Cornell University, Ithaca, New York.

FURNITURE CUTOUTS

Living Room

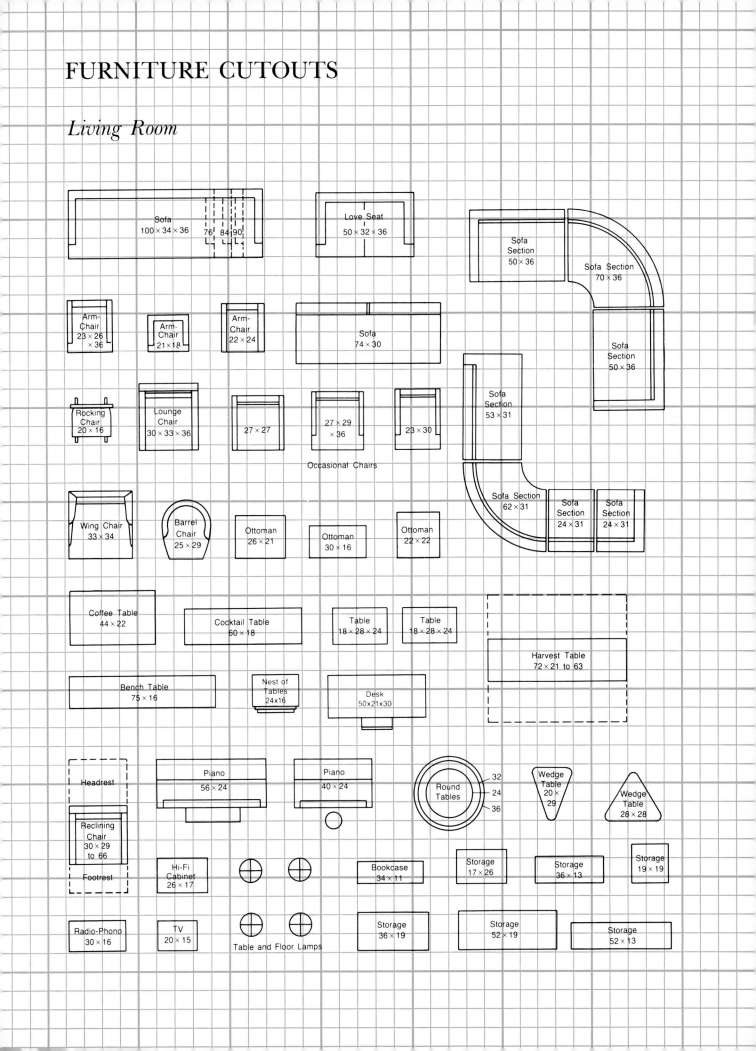

Sofa
100 × 34 × 36   76 84 90

Love Seat
50 × 32 × 36

Sofa
Section
50 × 36

Sofa Section
70 × 36

Arm-
Chair
23 × 26
× 36

Arm-
Chair
21 × 18

Arm-
Chair
22 × 24

Sofa
74 × 30

Sofa
Section
50 × 36

Rocking
Chair
20 × 16

Lounge
Chair
30 × 33 × 36

27 × 27

27 × 29
× 36

23 × 30

Sofa
Section
53 × 31

Occasional Chairs

Wing Chair
33 × 34

Barrel
Chair
25 × 29

Ottoman
26 × 21

Ottoman
30 × 16

Ottoman
22 × 22

Sofa Section
62 × 31

Sofa
Section
24 × 31

Sofa
Section
24 × 31

Coffee Table
44 × 22

Cocktail Table
60 × 18

Table
18 × 28 × 24

Table
18 × 28 × 24

Harvest Table
72 × 21 to 63

Bench Table
75 × 16

Nest of
Tables
24 × 16

Desk
50 × 21 × 30

Headrest

Piano
56 × 24

Piano
40 × 24

Round
Tables

32
24
36

Wedge
Table
20 ×
29

Wedge
Table
28 × 28

Reclining
Chair
30 × 29
to 66

Hi-Fi
Cabinet
26 × 17

Bookcase
34 × 11

Storage
17 × 26

Storage
36 × 13

Storage
19 × 19

Footrest

Radio-Phono
30 × 16

TV
20 × 15

Table and Floor Lamps

Storage
36 × 19

Storage
52 × 19

Storage
52 × 13

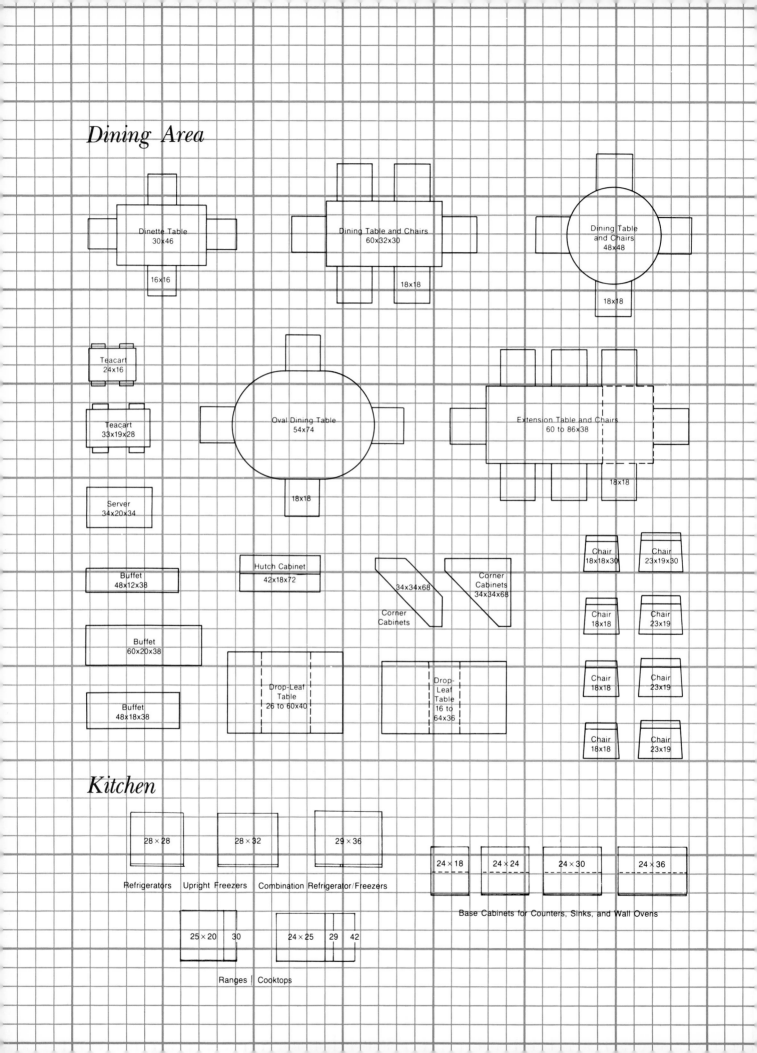

Dining Area

Dinette Table
30x46

16x16

Dining Table and Chairs
60x32x30

18x18

Dining Table
and Chairs
48x48

18x18

Teacart
24x16

Teacart
33x19x28

Oval Dining Table
54x74

18x18

Extension Table and Chairs
60 to 86x38

18x18

Server
34x20x34

Hutch Cabinet
42x18x72

34x34x68

Corner
Cabinets
34x34x68

Corner
Cabinets

Chair
18x18x30

Chair
23x19x30

Buffet
48x12x38

Chair
18x18

Chair
23x19

Buffet
60x20x38

Drop-Leaf
Table
26 to 60x40

Drop-
Leaf
Table
16 to
64x36

Chair
18x18

Chair
23x19

Buffet
48x18x38

Chair
18x18

Chair
23x19

Kitchen

28 × 28

28 × 32

29 × 36

24 × 18

24 × 24

24 × 30

24 × 36

Refrigerators   Upright Freezers   Combination Refrigerator/Freezers

Base Cabinets for Counters, Sinks, and Wall Ovens

25 × 20   30

24 × 25   29   42

Ranges | Cooktops

Bedroom

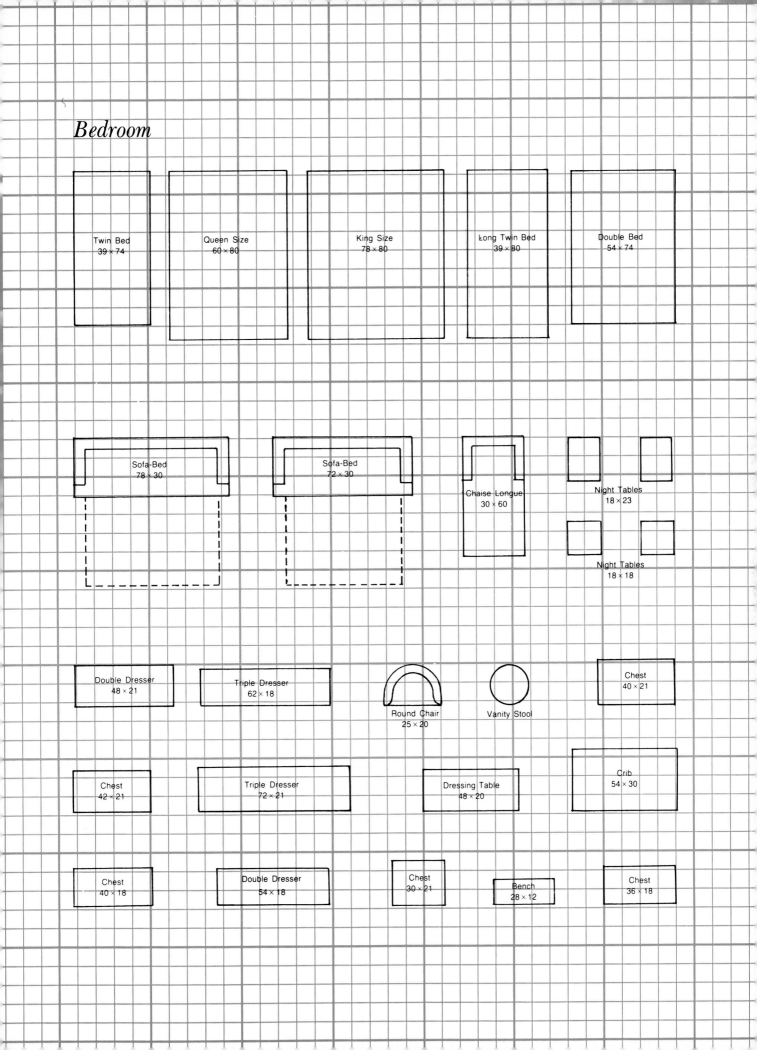

Twin Bed
39 × 74

Queen Size
60 × 80

King Size
78 × 80

Long Twin Bed
39 × 80

Double Bed
54 × 74

Sofa-Bed
78 × 30

Sofa-Bed
72 × 30

Chaise Longue
30 × 60

Night Tables
18 × 23

Night Tables
18 × 18

Double Dresser
48 × 21

Triple Dresser
62 × 18

Round Chair
25 × 20

Vanity Stool

Chest
40 × 21

Chest
42 × 21

Triple Dresser
72 × 21

Dressing Table
48 × 20

Crib
54 × 30

Chest
40 × 18

Double Dresser
54 × 18

Chest
30 × 21

Bench
28 × 12

Chest
36 × 18

Index